THE NOBLE TASK

THE ELDER

*A Practical Manual for the Operation of the Church
Session in the Presbyterian Church in the United States*

by Andrew A. Jumper

JOHN KNOX PRESS
Richmond, Virginia

To my fathers and brethren in the Lord, of the past, the present, and the future, who, serving our Saviour with wisdom, integrity, and faithfulness, fulfill their noble task, thereby making His Church great.

"The saying is sure: If any one aspires to the office of bishop, he desires a noble task" (1 Timothy 3:1).

Revised Edition, 1965
Fifth Printing, 1966

Library of Congress Catalog Card Number: 65-14420
© M. E. Bratcher 1961
Revised Edition © M. E. Bratcher 1965
Printed in the United States of America
J.4387

Preface

The Session of the local church is the heart of our denomination and of our system of government. One never feels that he has the final or even the best word on the work of the Session. Its responsibilities are so many and varied, the ways of performing them so numerous, that one small book could not begin to encompass them all or do justice to even a few of them. Therefore, the author's hope is that those who use this book will do so prudently and judiciously.

Much has been written about the office of the Elder and its nature. However, our efforts here are along a somewhat different line. There seems to be a real need in many Sessions for some structuring and guidance in fulfilling the noble task that is ours as Teaching and Ruling Elders. This little book is an effort to meet that need.

I wish to express my deep appreciation to the Ruling Elders of Christ Presbyterian Church, Houston, Texas, and West Shore Presbyterian Church, Dallas, Texas, for all I have learned from them, both in the things of the Church and in the ways of the Lord. They have been my patient teachers, my kind and wise counselors, and—best of all—my friends in Christ.

Thanks are also due to that seminary professor who first stirred my interest and guided my initial thinking along these lines, Dr. James A. Millard, Jr., who is now the Stated Clerk of the General Assembly; to the Rev. Henry W. Quinius, Jr., of Austin Presbyterian Theological Seminary, who has made materials available to me and given encouragement; and to our office staff at West Shore, who have protected me as much as possible so as to provide time for the writing of this book.

Last, but by no means least, deep appreciation goes to my wife, Elizabeth. She has corrected my spelling, punctuated my sentences, done the final typing, and made valuable suggestions and criticisms—all in addition to caring for our home and our four children. Without her, not a word would have been written, for her love and encouragement have always been my inspiration.

ANDREW A. JUMPER

Preface to the Revised Edition

Revising this manual in accordance with the new structures recommended by the Inter-Agency Committee of our Assembly has not been as difficult as writing the original manuscript, but it has had its frustrations! I wish to express appreciation to my friend Wayne Muse who let me ventilate my frustrations to him without letting me take myself too seriously, to my staff at the First Presbyterian Church, Lubbock, Texas, for protecting me while rewriting, and to my personal secretary, Mrs. J. M. Moore, who supervised the necessary typing.

ANDREW A. JUMPER

Contents

I

THE OFFICE OF
THE RULING ELDER

Its Nature and Origin

So you are a Ruling Elder! That means you now hold the highest honor and office that your church can bestow upon you. There is no office in the Presbyterian Church which, by its nature, is higher than the one you now hold. The origins of your office go far back into the history of Israel, at least to the time of Moses, as we see in Exodus 18:25, where we read: "Moses chose able men out of all Israel, and made them heads over the people . . ." (See also Exodus 18:13-27. Indications are that this office may go back even further. See particularly Exodus 3:16 and 12:21.) The Book of Church Order puts it this way:

> As there were Elders of the people for the government of the Old Testament Church, so under the New Testament Christ has furnished others beside the Ministers of the Word with gifts and commission to govern when called thereunto. These officers are the Ruling Elders.[1]

In New Testament times, as early as the days of Paul, the election of Elders to govern is already well established. Thus we find Paul instructing a young pastor named Titus:

> ". . . appoint elders in every town as I directed you, men who are blameless, married only once, whose children are believers and not open to the charge of being profligate or insubordinate. For a bishop, as God's steward, must be blameless . . ." (see Titus 1:5-7).

---

1. *The Book of Church Order of the Presbyterian Church in the United States,* Revised Edition (Richmond, Virginia: John Knox Press, 1963), Section 11-1. (Sections are indicated by the symbol §.)

The Greek word "presbuteros," which is translated "elder," originally meant "old man." By New Testament times, however, it had come to mean also one who was wise, mature, and capable of sound judgment. Thus, as the word "elder" is used in the New Testament it means one who is mature in the faith and is wise and of sound judgment in the things of the Lord. Our word "Presbyterian" means, literally, "rule by Elders."

The word "elder" speaks to us of maturity, of wisdom, of stability, of dignity, of broad experience. Surely this is something of what Paul means when he writes:

> "Now a bishop must be above reproach, the husband of one wife, temperate, sensible, dignified, hospitable, an apt teacher, no drunkard, not violent but gentle, not quarrelsome, and no lover of money. He must manage his own household well, keeping his children submissive and respectful in every way; for if a man does not know how to manage his own household, how can he care for God's church? He must not be a recent convert, or he may be puffed up with conceit and fall into the condemnation of the devil; moreover he must be well thought of by outsiders, or he may fall into reproach and the snare of the devil" (1 Timothy 3:2-7).

To be called "Elder" says something of your life and character, of your reputation both in the church and in the community. Yours, then, is a high and holy calling; it is an exacting and demanding responsibility. As you begin—or continue—your years of service in this divine calling, you will want to think through some of the responsibilities that are yours.

You will want to remember always that whereas your office is one of honor and esteem, it is most of all an office of responsibility. As the Book of Church Order puts it, "It belongs to their [the elders'] office, both individually and jointly, to watch diligently over the congregation committed to their charge . . ." (§ 11-4).

To be called an Elder also speaks to you of the manner of your daily life. In the sense that we commonly use the word, you are no longer a layman. You have been called to office by the people of God; you have felt God's call yourself; and you have been approved by a court of the Church (§ 23-1). As the Session laid its hands upon you, you were set apart. You were ordained by this ancient and sacred rite to the office of Ruling Elder. From this time forward your entire relationship to the Church and its work is no longer a matter of choice or convenience; it is now a matter of covenant—between you and your God, between you and your church, and between you and your fellow officers. As Paul once charged Timothy, so he charges you: "As for you, always be steady, endure suffering . . . fulfil your ministry" (2 Timothy 4:5).

In a very real sense, you are now the representative of your congregation. Not only do you represent them in the work of the Church; you represent them to the world. In every area of life, whether at home, at church, at play, or at work, your Saviour and your people are being judged by who and what you are. Never forget that every act is now, in the deepest sense of the word, a silent sermon to the world on the depth of your faith, the sincerity of your profession, and the love which you bear to the one whom you call Lord. Although you have rights, privileges, and freedoms as a person and a Christian, remember the example of Christ,

> ". . . who, though he was in the form of God, did not count equality with God a thing to be grasped, but emptied himself, taking the form of a servant, being born in the likeness of men. And being found in human form he humbled himself and became obedient unto death, even death on a cross" (Philippians 2:6-8).

Being an Elder has many implications for you. It speaks not only of your responsibility in attendance at services of worship and at meetings of the Session, but also of your fulfillment of duties as you serve on committees and as you oversee the flock of God. It would be impossible to list them all! But you will serve the Lord well and faithfully if, in all you do, you seek to follow Christ, as did Paul, who could say, "Be imitators of me, as I am of Christ" (1 Corinthians 11:1).

Qualifications for Office

In Section 11-3, the Book of Church Order says:

> Those who fill this office should be blameless in life and sound in the faith, men of wisdom and discretion. By the holiness of their walk and conversation they should be examples of Christian faith.

Those two brief, pungent sentences are simply put, but they cover much. The qualifications for office speak of the blamelessness of your life, which has to do with your Christian character as it finds daily expression. It speaks of the soundness of your faith, which has to do with the integrity and truth of what you believe. The idea that it doesn't matter what you believe so long as you are sincere is far from true. As one who is enjoined to be apt to teach the Word (§ 11-4); who may be called upon to fill the pulpit from time to time; who is to "instruct the ignorant" (§ 11-4); and who is to "watch diligently over the congregation committed to [his] charge, that no corruption of doctrine or of morals enter therein" (§ 11-4), you will need to be "sound in the faith" (§ 11-3).

The qualifications for office speak also of "wisdom and discretion" (§ 11-3). Hasty, ill-advised actions have no place in the church, whose mission stretches beyond time (Ephesians 2:7). Sometimes a church is criticized for acting and moving so slowly. Yet wisdom and discretion often demand reflection and study that come with time. An Elder must put aside any personal motivations and individual ambitions when it comes to the work of the church. He must be wise and discreet.

The qualifications for office speak of your "walk and conversation" (§ 11-3). That is a good, old-fashioned way of speaking of the way you live. To us today, the word "conversation" means primarily talking, which is certainly a part of it. A Christian is careful of what he says and how he says it. But the meaning of the word in this phrase is much broader than that. It has to do with the whole of life and the way it is lived. So the qualifications for the office of Elder put the responsibility squarely upon you: they speak of purity of character, of the soundness of faith, and of wisdom and discretion (§ 11-3). They speak of the holiness that permeates the whole of life and serves as an example to all men (§ 11-3). No one can truly say that it is easy to be an Elder. As Paul once put it, "The saying is sure: If any one aspires to the office of bishop, he desires a noble task" (1 Timothy 3:1). As you serve in the church as one ordained, set apart by the laying on of hands, be diligent to fulfill your high and holy calling, for it is indeed a noble task.

Preparation for Service

The fact that you have been elected by the congregation to the office of Elder and have been ordained by your Session says something about you. It testifies to your Christian character, to your faithfulness, and to the esteem in which you are held by your fellow Christians and church members. But you will discover that others now look to you for information and facts, knowledge and understanding, which perhaps were not expected before. You will be expected to live and act on quite a new level. Let us think together for a moment of some of these things as you prepare yourself more adequately for this "noble task."

First, there is your home life. When you read 1 Timothy 3:1-7 and Titus 1:5-9, you discover that Paul laid tremendous emphasis upon the home life of the Elder (or Bishop, which is another Biblical term for Elder). You will remember that even in Old Testament times the home was the central religious unit among the Hebrews, both for training and living. The head of the house was responsible for the religious life of his family as well as for their training in the doctrines of their faith. We are realizing more fully now that the home has the primary responsibility for Christian nurture and that the relationships and attitudes in the home are significant factors affecting Christian growth. You will want to think through some of the things necessary to make your home an effective unit of Christian learning and experience.

Family worship is an important part of this duty. As an officer and a Christian, you need the spiritual strength that comes through the study of God's Word and the inspiration and guidance that come through prayer. There are many helps available to guide you in conducting family worship. Our Board of Christian Education publishes a quarterly devotional booklet entitled *Day by Day* and many other helps. Your church probably provides these; if not, you can order from the Presbyterian Book Store nearest you.[2] If you have small children, you may want to use material especially adapted for them. Lists of the materials and books available can be secured from your Presbyterian Book Store. But whatever material you use, make certain that you and your family worship together regularly.

Worship at church is, of course, intimately connected with worship at home. There, as the people of God gather together, God comes to them in a very special way. Through the preaching of the Word and the administration of the sacraments, God speaks to His people. You will need this source of inspiration and strength. Although no member should miss stated services of worship unless—to use a good Presbyterian phrase—he is "providentially hindered," this responsibility is particularly incumbent upon an Elder. There is nothing more discouraging and disheartening to a congregation and the pastor than to have officers who are not faithful and exemplary in their attendance and support of services of worship. You, along with your fellow officers, must take the lead always.

You should also be apt to teach. You need not only the learning that comes from home and church, but also the additional opportunity presented to you through the adult classes of your church school. When a Christian stops growing in his knowledge and in his faith and understanding, he runs the serious risk of spiritual stagnation. Every opportunity for learning should be followed, to the end that you may be enabled to take an active part in the teaching ministry of the church in whatever group your talents can best be used.

---

2. Box 6127, Atlanta, Georgia 30308.
118 W. Fifth Street, Charlotte, N. C. 28202, serving Charlotte and vicinity. (No mail orders are handled in Charlotte.)
Box 1020, Dallas, Texas 75221.
Box 1176, Richmond, Virginia 23209.

Aside from worship and study, you will be expected to know what is going on in your church. There are several things you can do to prepare yourself in this area. Since you are charged, along with your fellow Elders, with the spiritual oversight of your congregation, one of the first things you will want to do is to make a determined effort to *know* your fellow church members. Get out your church roll and make a check by the name of every person you know; and then set out to meet and know by sight and name those whom you do not know. Do not stop until every name in your roll book has a check by it! Then, as new members join the church, make yourself known to them. Make a point of speaking to them each Sunday and making them feel welcome and at home. They are seeking to find a place for themselves in your church family, and the fact that you know them and are concerned and interested in them will help. Too, they are more likely to turn to you as their spiritual guide and counselor in time of trouble if they know you care about them.

Another thing you will want to do is to study your church paper or news sheet. It will tell you things you will want to remember about people, and it will give you a picture of the total program of the church. It will be impossible to take part in all the activities of the church; but as an Elder you should be concerned to know what is going on, what is being done, and who is doing it.

As never before, you are now concerned with more than the local church. Your responsibilities as an Elder compel you to have a concern that reaches out into your Presbytery, your Synod, and your General Assembly. You will want to know what other churches are doing and what other people are thinking about the same problems that confront you in your church. Many Presbyteries publish a monthly or quarterly news sheet. Find out about it and subscribe to the one in your Presbytery. (Usually there is no cost, and it will merely be a matter of getting your name on the mailing list.) Most Synods now have some sort of paper that is published regularly. You will want to subscribe so that you can be familiar with the plans and hopes of the Church and with the accomplishments and ideas of others. If your church does not subscribe to the *Presbyterian Survey* on the "Every Family Plan" or the "Church Leaders' Plan," you should subscribe on an individual basis at once.[3] This is the only official magazine of our General Assembly; it will be of invaluable help to you. In addition, you should subscribe to one of the independent church papers.[4] There you will find helpful analysis of problems and issues that face the Church. These papers make a very real contribution to the life of the Church by objective criticism and appraisal of important events and will help you gain a better-rounded perspective. As a well-read, well-informed officer, you will be a genuine asset to your local church as you take part in its work, plans, and growth.

In the past you may have heard a great deal about Presbytery and the other courts of your Church. Now, in a far different sense, you will be concerned about the work of these courts. The Book of Church Order states in Section 11-2 that Ruling Elders, together with Teaching Elders (ministers),

> . . . take the oversight of the spiritual interests both of the particular church and of the Church generally when appointed to represent their churches in the higher courts. In all the courts of the Church these Ruling Elders possess the same authority and the same eligibility to office as the Ministers of the Word.

As a Ruling Elder, you will have opportunity from time to time to represent your church at meetings of Presbytery and Synod. The time may also come when you will be elected a Commissioner from your Presbytery to a meeting of the General Assembly. Take advantage of these opportunities. You will be thrilled and inspired to see our Church at work and to know how effectively our Biblical form of government works. Through

---

3. *Presbyterian Survey*, 341 Ponce de Leon Ave., N. E., Atlanta, Georgia 30308. Subscription rates: Individuals—1 year, $3; 2 years, $5; 3 years, $7. "Every Family Plan" available to churches—$1 a year per family. "Church Leaders' Plan" available to churches—$1.50 a year per church leader.
4. *The Presbyterian Outlook*, 512 East Main St., Richmond, Virginia 23219. $5 a year.
The Christian Observer, 412 South Third St., Louisville, Kentucky 40202. $4 a year ($3 for ministers).
The Presbyterian Journal, Weaverville, North Carolina 28787. $3 a year for individuals, $2 a year for Every Family Plan churches.

the various church papers you can keep up with the work of these courts and be an informed and wise representative when your time comes to attend. Other Ruling Elders from your church will report to the Session their attendance at Presbytery and the actions taken there. Be alert to keep up with these actions and the work of the Church.

Perhaps a word should be said at this point about your continuing education as an Elder in the Presbyterian Church. Probably your pastor led you through the required instruction on the Confession of Faith[5] and the Book of Church Order prior to your examination by the Session (§ 15-6 (6)). In any event, before your ordination you were required to know something about the faith of our Church and its organizational structure. However, this was not the end of the matter but its beginning. With the passage of time, you will discover that you have forgotten many of the things you learned; some things were only half learned, some things were mislearned, and some were never learned! What you have actually had is only an introduction; now the real task of learning begins. You should read and study your Confession of Faith regularly and systematically. As questions arise, discuss them with your pastor and fellow Elders.[6] You should, after a time, be able to quote from it, even as you do favorite passages of Scripture. A consecrated and earnest Session might well spend a few minutes at the beginning of each meeting discussing some great doctrine of faith as it is set forth in our Standards. Also, as you work on the Session many questions about procedure, areas of responsibility, etc., will arise. Therefore, a continued study of the Book of Church Order is not only helpful but necessary. Every good Presbyterian officer has in addition to his Bible these two books, each of which should become well-worn from continued use.

Further, you the Elder are responsible for helping the congregation to understand the needs of people in the community

---

5. *The Confession of Faith of the Presbyterian Church in the United States,* Revised (Richmond, Virginia: John Knox Press, 1965).

6. A helpful analysis and interpretation of our Presbyterian doctrine is found in *The Westminster Confession for Today* by George S. Hendry (Richmond, Virginia: John Knox Press, 1960).

beyond the bounds of the congregation. Not only so, but you have the responsibility for helping the congregation to know the causes of human need and to act in eliminating these causes. This will mean that you will have to be aware of the social problems which so vitally affect the welfare of all people within the geographical area of the congregation and beyond. God is no respecter of persons in His concern for human welfare. You as an ordained servant of God must manifest His concern for all people.

There is one final thing to be said, which concerns your stewardship. We all know that being a Christian demands a stewardship of all of life, including our material goods. As an officer in the Church of Jesus Christ and as one charged with the solemn responsibility of being "examples of Christian faith" (§ 11-3), you will want to give of your goods to the Lord. Our Church teaches that whereas the tithe (ten percent of all income) is not an end in itself, it is a proper starting point and a means to growth in commitment (see Minutes of the General Assembly, 1961, page 132). No officer should be content until he is making a full stewardship of that which God has entrusted to him. As an Elder you will be planning programs and setting policies that will be financed by members of your congregation. Surely no true Elder would think of directing the giving of others unless he himself is committed to an all-inclusive stewardship. Surely for an Elder the tithe is not the end of his giving but the beginning, as he "gives freely and increasingly and of abundant joy" (Minutes of the General Assembly, 1961, page 132).

So when you are worshiping God regularly both at home and at church; when you are studying systematically the Word of God; when you are well informed about the total program of the Church; when you are continuing to grow in your understanding of the Constitution of our Church; and when you are setting a well-rounded example of the Christian faith, particularly in the realm of giving, as an Elder you are on the road to fulfilling your "noble task."

II

THE CHURCH SESSION
THE BOARD OF DEACONS
AND THE TASK

The Session and the Board of Deacons can have a happy and harmonious working relationship together. However, this is possible only when both clearly and fully understand the areas of work and responsibility that belong to each. Before we can talk about organizing for our task as a Session, we need first of all to fix firmly in our minds the relationship between these two bodies and to determine the areas of responsibility that belong respectively to the Board and the Session. At the same time we should determine the place of the pastor and his unique relationship to the Session.

The Session's Responsibility for the Life and Work of the Church

In many churches the idea seems to prevail that the Session is responsible for the spiritual life of the congregation whereas the Board of Deacons is charged with the care of the congregation's material and financial life, and never the twain shall meet! Nothing could be less true. According to the Book of Church Order, the Session is charged with the oversight of the *total* life and work of the church, which includes its material and financial aspects. The Book of Church Order states in Section 12-5, "As the whole church is under the jurisdiction of the Session, the Deacons, in the discharge of their duties, are under the supervision and authority of the Session." This means that the Board of Deacons is responsible not directly to the congregation but to the Session. Thus, our Book of Church Order says: "The regular budget and other important financial matters require the approval of the Session" (§ 12-3); the Board ". . . shall submit its minutes to the Session at least once every six months and at other times upon the request of the Session" (§ 12-4); the Board shall meet "whenever requested by the Session" (§ 12-4); and "If it seems necessary or wise for the best interest of the church, the Session may void or amend any action of the Board of Deacons, or return it to them for further consideration" (§ 12-5). We see further indications of the responsibility of the Session in the following statement: "In a church in which Deacons can not be secured, the duties of the office shall devolve upon the Ruling Elders" (§ 12-5).

Very simply, this means that our form of government provides a system of "checks and balances" for its operation in order that those who are ultimately responsible may properly fulfill their task. Thus, the Church Session has the responsibility of review and control over the work of the Board of Deacons, somewhat as the Presbytery does over the Session. This does not mean that the Session will ordinarily override the work of the Board. As a matter of fact, a diligent, consecrated Session rarely overrules the actions of a Board that is faithfully trying to do its work, even though a Session might sometimes feel that a particular action is neither wise nor judicious. But our Presbyterian system does put the responsibility where it finally belongs, on the shoulders of the Session.

The Book of Church Order states that the Ruling Elders are the "immediate representatives of the people" (§ 11-2). Although the members of the Board of Deacons are elected by the congregation, no such statement is made concerning their representation. Rather, our system of government makes them directly responsible to the Session. The Deacons are immediately responsible for a particular area of work, which we shall examine in a moment; but the Session is ultimately responsible for the total program of the church, which includes the work of the Board of Deacons.

The Work of the Board of Deacons

According to the Book of Church Order, the area of responsibility of the Board is definitely set forth and limited. We read in Section 12-3:

> It is the duty of the Deacons, first of all, to minister to those who are in need, to the sick, to the friendless, and to any who may be in distress. It is their further duty to develop the grace of liberality in the members of the church; to plan, in collaboration with the Session, the objects toward which the offerings of the congregation shall regularly be directed; to plan effective methods for gathering these offerings; to receive other offerings as directed by the Session; and to see that all offerings are distributed among the objects toward which they have been contributed. It is their duty also to have the care of the property of the congregation, both real and personal, and to keep in proper repair the church edifice and other buildings belonging to the congregation.

We might break this down into four primary areas of responsibility—first, to exercise the ministry of compassion on behalf of the congregation; second, to develop the grace of liberality in the members; third, to collect, record, and disburse according to plan the finances of the church; fourth, to care for and keep up the properties of the church.* This means that the Board of Deacons has no independent authorization to work or act, save in these areas. It also means that even within the framework of these specific areas, the Board is directly responsible to the Session for its faithfulness and diligence. The Session may, for the best interests of the church, void or amend or send back for consideration any action of the Board. A wise Session will of course always be reluctant to act in these areas and will be careful to consult with the Board; but it must always be remembered that the Session is still ultimately responsible for the total program and work of the church, which includes the work assigned to the Board of Deacons.

---

* For a fuller description of the work and organization of the Board of Deacons, see *Chosen to Serve* by Andrew A. Jumper (Richmond, Virginia: John Knox Press, 1961).

The Task of the Session

The area of responsibility for the Session is broader and much more difficult to define. The Book of Church Order lays down some specific items of power (and responsibility) in Section 15-6. However, closer study will reveal that each of these items is in reality a broad principle that gives rise to duties and responsibilities other than those specifically stated. For our purposes, let us set forth the major areas of responsibility. In subsequent chapters we shall deal with these sweeping principles in detail.

The Book of Church Order is very wise in laying down only broad, general principles of responsibility for the local church. Each church will differ according to size, locality, and a variety of other factors. It would be impossible to lay down specific duties that would fit every local need or situation. Therefore, the Book of Church Order attempts to point us in the direction of our responsibility, laying down some general principles and areas of responsibility and leaving the details to each local Session. Fundamentally the areas of responsibility are: worship, commitment, witness, service, and strengthening the church for these tasks. These are further summarized for us in Section 9-2, where we read:

> The whole polity of the Church consists of (1) doctrine, including worship and the administration of the Sacraments, (2) government, including discipline, and (3) distribution, the Church's ministry of compassion.

We shall be looking at each of these areas in detail in subsequent chapters. We might think now of these areas in terms of the life of an individual Christian. The Session would be responsible for providing him opportunities to glorify God through worship; for leading him to a real and deep commitment; for helping him give expression to that commitment through witnessing and service; and for nurturing him in the Christian faith and life.

The Session and the Pastor

The pastor *is* a member of the Session who has all the rights and privileges, as well as responsibilities, that any other Elder has; and this includes voting on all matters (§ 15-1). He is the Moderator of the Session (§ 15-1) and has the power to convene the Session whenever he deems it necessary (§ 15-5); and the Session may not meet without him except in case of emergency (§ 15-5 and § 15-3). This means that the pastor has the right to voice his opinions and state his convictions on issues that come before the Session. On the other hand, it does not mean that he may control the actions of the Session or dictate to them on any matter (§ 9-3). Teaching and Ruling Elders jointly exercise the power of the Church, which is called the Power of Jurisdiction (§ 1-4). However, it is to be remembered that the minister (Teaching Elder) exercises, under the Power of Order, certain powers that belong to him individually by virtue of office, particularly preaching and the administration of the sacraments (§ 1-4).

What does this mean for the Session in practical application? It means that the minister is a very real part of the Session and serves in a key position as its Moderator. However, the most important thing is not actually stated in the Book of Church Order, but only implied and inferred. As the minister, laboring uniquely in the Word, he is in a strategic position to assist the Session and to give them sound advice on matters under discussion. Use his advice well. Do not be a rubber stamp, but judiciously weigh the value of his knowledge, his concern, and his experience. Then, in the light of the best advice and evidence, vote your earnest, sincere convictions.

Perhaps a suggestion should be made at this point to the Ruling Elders. As the group closest to the pastor, you should also offer him the benefit of your counsel and advice. You should keep him informed on matters coming to your attention which he should know and which affect the life and work of the church. Your pastor carries a large responsibility upon his shoulders. Be quick to help, defend, uphold, and encourage him. As far as it is possible, let your Church Session offer your pastor a ministry of love, sympathy, understanding, and compassion to sustain and strengthen him in his ministry to the church. Be a pastor to your pastor; he has no other. Most important, remember him daily in your prayers.

Joint Meetings of the Session and Board of Deacons

The Book of Church Order does not require that the Session and Board meet in joint session; but it does state: "It is desirable that the Session and the Board of Deacons meet in joint session once a quarter to confer on matters of common interest" (§ 12-5). Every Church Session should follow this sound advice. As Elders and Deacons sit down together to discuss the work and program of the church, the knotty problems that each church often faces can be worked out. When tensions and frictions arise between the two official bodies, usually it is due to a lack of communication and understanding. In joint meetings Elders and Deacons can get to know one another better. By mutual love and exchange of ideas, by mutual trust and sharing, the Kingdom of God is served and advanced. Always remember that the Deacons lean heavily on your experience and wisdom as well as upon the maturity of your faith and the spiritual depth of your counsel. Remember, too, that sometimes the Deacons are not as wise in the ways of the Lord as the Elders. Frequently they are younger and newer in the faith. This means that you may often be called upon to guide or give advice without extinguishing the enthusiasm and initiative of younger persons. You yourself may, in turn, be stimulated by their vigorous enthusiasm.

A word should be said at this point regarding actions taken at a joint officers' meeting. The Book of Church Order states in Section 12-5: "The joint meeting can make no binding decision, but the Session and Board of Deacons can act separately on matters committed to the care of each." As far as "legality" goes, the minutes of a joint officers' meeting are not worth very much, for neither the Board nor the Session is officially bound by such actions. Some Sessions "legalize" joint actions by adopting resolutions made in joint meetings; but they are not bound to do so. This means that although a Session might feel morally bound to such decisions, its jurisdiction over the Board of Deacons is not voided. As a member of the Session, you will want to keep faith with joint decisions and actions as far as possible; but you must not use this as an excuse for abdicating your responsibility as an Elder and a member of the Church Session.

The Session and the Congregation

There has been confusion from time to time in most Sessions over the concept of representation. Our form of church government is the representative form. Does this mean that the Elder is to discover the desires of members of the congregation and vote in accordance with their wishes? Some have thought so. However, this violates the very nature of our government and is but a disguised form of congregationalism. To represent means to act for or in the place of. A responsible Elder is one who represents his congregation by voting his own convictions that arise out of his faith and his desire to be obedient to the mind of Christ. In some instances this may cut across the wishes of the majority of the congregation. Yet, the Elder not only represents the people; he also represents Jesus Christ, and his decisions must be guided by a higher loyalty and representation. You are an Elder because you are "wise and discreet." As such you are to use your best knowledge and understanding and to vote your sincere convictions.

Does the congregation retain any "control" over Elders and the Session? Only to the extent that it may *request* the Session to dissolve "the active relationship between the church and the officer" (§ 29-8), and that it must give its consent "in matters of special importance affecting the property of the church" (§ 12-3). Other rights reserved to the congregation include calling a pastor (§ 25-2), changing the terms of a pastor's call (with the consent of Presbytery) (§ 25-2), the election of officers (§§ 23-1, 23-2, and 29-1) and related matters such as establishing limited terms of service (§ 29-11). Also, it is possible for a congregation to deal with any matter by presenting to the Session a written request, signed by one-fourth of the congregation, that a congregational meeting be called for that purpose (§ 5-2). On the other hand, since the Session will be expecting the congrega-

tion to participate in certain programs and work, there are
occasions when a wise Session will ask a congregation for its
concurrence and support; for example, in accepting the annual
budget of the church, and in supporting special services and
other important activities affecting the life of the church.

The Session and Matters of Policy

When we speak of areas of responsibility of the Session and
the Board, we must also speak of policy. By policy we mean any
action that is determinative of program and decides the direction in which the work and worship of the church shall go.
Therefore, since policy does determine program and since the
Session of the church is ultimately responsible for the total
program of the church, it naturally follows that the Session is the
policy-making body of the church. For example, money is always
a determining factor in program. How much money is set aside
for, say, the Committee on Strengthening the Church is going to
help determine what sort of educational program the church
will have. This is clearly a matter of policy and therefore falls
under the responsibility of the Session. Thus, the Book of
Church Order states in Section 12-3 that "the regular budget
and other important financial matters require the approval of
the Session." It further states that the authority of the Board of
Deacons to disburse funds is limited in that the funds are to be
"distributed among the objects toward which they have been
contributed" (§ 12-3).

Let us look at several illustrations of how the matter of policy
works and how the responsibilities of the Session and the Board
are clearly separated at this point. For example, suppose the
Session determines that additional staff or office personnel is
needed. Who determines working hours, salary, vacation, etc.?
These are clearly matters of policy and rightly belong to the
responsibility and authority of the Session. The wise Session will
consult with the Board of Deacons concerning funds available
and will also ask for their suggestions; but the ultimate decision
on these matters rests with the Session since these are matters
of policy.

Suppose again that the financial income of the church is insufficient to meet budgeted needs. Who determines which items shall be cut or omitted? Who decides what committees must suffer in their program? This is clearly a matter of policy and is a function of the Session. Again, the Church Session will surely want to consult with the Board of Deacons; but no consecrated Session would attempt to avoid the responsibility for such a decision.

When friction arises between Session and Board it can usually be traced to a confusion of policy-making decisions and responsibilities. It is the duty of the Session to make the policies and to keep the Board informed of any policy action that affects the work of the Board. Communication is a real problem at this point, and every Session must handle it realistically. We will have more to say on this when we come to discuss the stewardship responsibilities of the Session. But let it be clearly understood that the policy-making power and responsibility are lodged with the Session. Let it also be remembered that the Board of Deacons has no discretionary powers in terms of policy. The alert Session will be diligent to see that policy matters are clearly stated and that all are informed of these policies. As new items arise, the Session will be quick to establish policies that will guide the direction and content of the program of the church.

The Session's relationship to pastor, to congregation, and to the Board of Deacons may seem a complicated and difficult one. It calls for tact and diplomacy; it requires patience and restraint; it demands Christian love and understanding. But the noble task to which you are called is worth the effort. Give it the time and attention it deserves, that the task may indeed be nobly done!

III

ORGANIZING
FOR THE TASK

Sometimes a meeting of the Session may last far into the evening; yet in spite of the time spent together, often little seems to be accomplished. Frequently the reason for this is inadequate planning and poor organization. When every matter must be discussed at length by every Elder, when no one has any specific data or information, when no one has clearly stated the need to be met and the way of meeting that need, then it is almost inevitable that there will be confusion and "fuzziness" in thinking. Debates will be long and drawn out, with no apparent object in view. Therefore, if the Session is properly to fulfill its responsibilities and do its work with "wisdom and discretion," with dispatch and efficiency, it must properly organize itself for the noble task that belongs to it.

Because the needs of a church vary according to size, leadership, area, and a host of other factors, our Book of Church Order wisely refrains from structuring the Session except on very broad and general lines. However, there are some helps and suggestions available that we should be aware of. Let us digress for a moment to see where they come from, who produced them, and what they are.

Recent Developments in the Presbyterian Church

After the Second World War, we became conscious of changes occurring in Protestantism that had been brought about by developments in Biblical theology, psychology, education, and other related fields. As a result of these developments it became apparent that the times demanded a new look at the Church, particularly in the field of education.[1] As the Presbyterian Church, U. S., studied the implications of these developments, there came into being the Curriculum Improvement Program. This program dealt with the basic question, "Suppose we had no curriculum of Christian education whatsoever; what should we produce in order to communicate the gospel?" Out of a study of this question came what is now known as the "Covenant Life Curriculum."

With the new curriculum came another realization—that what we had learned through the Curriculum Improvement Program (CIP) had implications for the total life of the Church. We were no longer looking only at a new program of Christian education, but at the total life of the Church. The CIP study identified three aspects of the life of the Church which have a bearing on the educational work of the Church—the worship and work of the congregation, the family, and the school of the local church. It was clear that whereas the Board of Christian Education was responsible for providing resources for the church school and for family education, the worship and work of the congregation were the joint responsibility of all the Boards and Agencies of the General Assembly. Therefore, representatives of all of the Boards and Agencies of our General Assembly came together in a group called the Inter-Agency Committee. It was their job to develop and co-ordinate all of the aids, helps, and programs of the Assembly for the local congregation in its worship and work.

The first task of the IAC (Inter-Agency Committee) was to define "Worship and Work," and this has been done in a little book entitled "The Worship and Work of the Congregation."[2] This study saw the work of the local church falling into four areas: Commitment, Witness, Service, and Strengthening the Church. We now realized more clearly than ever before that the local church has one mission. All of the "programs" of the

1. For a summary of these developments, see "A Historical Statement" in the Appendix of *Education for Covenant Living*, beginning on page 111. Available from The CLC Press, Box 1176, Richmond, Va. 23209.
2. Available from your nearest Presbyterian Book Store, along with a guide entitled "Study Guide: The Worship and Work of the Congregation."

Church are in reality a part of that mission and should serve that mission. This fresh understanding made two things very clear. First, it made clear that the mission of the Church starts with the local congregation. Second, while it assumes that the work done through Assembly, Synod, and Presbytery agencies is a necessary part of the total work, it also made clear that their primary duty was to assist the local church in carrying out its mission in the world.

Through the Inter-Agency Committee at the Assembly level, our denomination now had a means of co-ordinating and unifying the various program aids, helps, and suggestions for the local church in order to serve it better as it fulfilled its mission. However, in order for the local congregation to take the best advantage of these suggestions, it became clear that we needed to re-think administration at the local level. Thus, the IAC produced a booklet entitled "A Suggested Guide for Administration in the Local Congregation."[3] Based on the four areas of Commitment, Witness, Service, and Strengthening the Church, this booklet offers suggested structures for Church Sessions of various sizes. In addition, it gives information that will be useful to a Session as it studies how it can best organize to do its task.

To organize properly will require some hard work and study; but there will be great dividends in terms of efficiency, time saved, and the assurance of duty fulfilled. This chapter will make organizational suggestions based on the Guide mentioned above; and in Appendix A may be found a sample of a Standard of Procedure.

Book of Church Order Requirements

The Book of Church Order requires that each Session have at least a limited organizational structure. It requires that the pastor be Moderator (§ 15-1 and § 13-2) and that the Church Session elect one of its members to serve as Clerk (§ 13-5). The

---

3. Available free from the Inter-Agency Committee, General Council, Presbyterian Church, U. S., 341 Ponce de Leon Avenue, N. E., Atlanta, Georgia 30308.

Book of Church Order further determines how often the Session must meet (at least quarterly, § 15-5), what its minimum quorum is (§ 15-2), and what basic records it must keep (§ 15-7 and § 15-8). In addition, it lays down many specific duties that are incumbent upon Elders in terms of Power of Order and Power of Jurisdiction (individual and collective). But there are many questions that the Book of Church Order does not answer. For example, the Clerk is elected for a definite period (§ 13-5); but when, for how long, and in what manner is he elected? In Section 15-6, our Book of Church Order lays down a long list of duties incumbent upon the Session; but specifically how does a Session go about fulfilling these duties? These are questions that are not answered for us, and rightly so. Each local situation is unique, and needs vary from Session to Session. It is left to each church to organize in the way that best suits its needs and through which it can best perform its task.

Obviously each Session will need certain committees and perhaps other officers, for the Moderator and Clerk could not possibly do everything. What officers are needed, and what will each do? If the Session must meet at least quarterly, when and where does it meet? Who determines the day and time? In order to answer these and many other questions that arise, this chapter will discuss organization, needs, and how to go about fulfilling the duties incumbent upon the Church Session.

The Standard of Procedure

Many Sessions do not have any official organizational structure or rules of procedure except in a very general way. Since Elders come and go—particularly where there is a system of limited service—and since times change and men forget, it is good for a diligent Session to set down the rules by which it will govern and organize itself and conduct its business. Such rules are called a Standard of Procedure. In such an organizational "manual" a Session sets down all the things that will guide it. In this way, the important and holy task of the Church Session is not left to chance or to the uncertain memory of man. Committees are indicated, duties are spelled out, rules are established, and procedure is delineated.

1. Officers to Be Elected

In setting up a Standard of Procedure, one of the first questions a Session must answer for itself is the number of officers it will need to elect to carry on its work. The Session must have a Moderator and a Clerk, for this is required by the Book of Church Order. (See Sections 15-3 and 15-4 for exceptions to the pastor's moderating when he is necessarily absent. See also Section 15-1, which deals with the moderatorship when there is an associate pastor.) However, to avoid confusion in time of emergency, a Session might desire to elect a Vice-Moderator, who would serve pro tempore in such instances. Also, it might like to elect an assistant Clerk. This would be particularly true in a larger Session where a great deal of business is handled. In any event, let the Session survey its needs and the possible eventualities that might arise and on this basis determine its most effective organization.

2. Establishing of Duties

Having determined what elected officers it will have, the Session must determine the duties of each officer and outline them fully.

3. Terms of Office and Election of Officers

The Session must next determine how long its officers (with the exception of the Moderator) shall serve, when they shall be elected, and how they shall be elected. We strongly recommend limited terms of office, with privilege of re-election for only one additional term. Sometimes a man becomes Clerk of the Session, for example, and continues to serve in that capacity year after year, even though his efficiency leaves much to be desired. Others are afraid of hurting his feelings or offending him. But when a limited term of office is provided in the Standard of Procedure, there is no room for hurt feelings. Also, other Elders with ability are given an opportunity to use their talents, and sometimes hidden talent is revealed. No person should have the right to feel that a particular job in the church "belongs" to him, year after year.

A definite time should be set for the election of officers. It may be advisable for them to be elected well in advance of their taking office, in order that each one may have time to prepare himself for the responsibility that is to be his. However, some Sessions may prefer to set up the new officers and committees after the newly elected Elders are ordained and installed. In this way the officers of the Session are chosen by the ones who actually will serve on it.

Yearly terms of a Sessional office should coincide with the time of installation of Elders. Otherwise, a Clerk of the Session elected for one year could be rotated off the Session before his term of service had expired.

Advance notification of election should be given in order that the members of the Session may know of the forthcoming election and may be considering suitable persons for the various offices. Since this is an important event in the life of the church, time is needed for deep consideration and earnest prayer as the Session chooses its leaders for another year.

4. *Method of Election of Church Session Officers*

In determining who will be nominated for office and how it is to be done, there are several possible methods from which to choose. Each Session can determine what method it will use, but that system should be used uniformly and consistently. One way is for the Moderator to appoint or the Session to elect a nominating committee for officers. (This system is particularly recommended if committee chairmen are elected.) This nominating committee should be named far enough in advance to give the members time to do their work thoroughly and well. Another method would be simply to have open nominations from the floor. Of course, even when a nominating committee is chosen, nominations may still be made from the floor.

5. *Vacancies or Absences in Essential Offices*

The American people are on the move! Population shifts, pro-
motions, job changes, and a host of other reasons send people
moving back and forth across our country. This means that from
time to time almost every Session will lose some of its members.
Death, sickness, and other unforeseen circumstances will cause
the loss of other Session members over a three-year period in almost every church. Therefore, the Session should be prepared
for such emergencies and should include in its Standard of Procedure a section that will specifically determine how the problem of vacancies in offices will be determined. Since every elective
position on the Session is important to the life of the church, it
might be wise to empower the Moderator to appoint someone to
fill the vacant office until such time as an election can be held.
When an officer is absent for an extended time because of illness,
business reasons, or other causes, the Moderator should be authorized to appoint someone to fill that office until the officer returns. Of course, in the case of sickness or other inability of the
Moderator to serve, the Vice-Moderator will serve unless conditions occur in which Section 15-3 or 15-4 of the Book of Church
Order would prevail. (See also the provisions of Section 15-1.)

6. *Meetings*

According to Section 15-5 of the Book of Church Order, the
Session shall meet at least quarterly for stated meetings. Most
churches will soon discover that this is not often enough when a
church is growing and expanding and the program is varied and
complex. However, each Session must determine how often it
should meet, as well as when and where. It would be wise for the
Session to set the stated monthly meeting (or however often the
Session determines to meet) on a specific day of the month, at a
specific place, and at a designated time. For example, the Session
might set the meeting as follows: "The Session shall ordinarily
meet on the third Monday of each month at 7:30 p.m. in the
Fellowship Hall of the church unless, at a regular stated meeting, by majority vote, the time and place of meeting shall other-

wise be set." Once a regular time, date, and place are established, the Elders will customarily reserve that date for the stated meeting of the Church Session. Also, if the church members know when the Session meets, other activities which might conflict with the meeting of the Session will not be scheduled for that day.

It is to be remembered that called meetings of the Session are to be held when deemed necessary by the Moderator (§ 15-5), or when directed by Presbytery (§ 15-5), or when requested by at least two Ruling Elders (§ 15-5), or when requested by one-fourth of the congregation for the purpose of calling a congregational meeting (§ 5-2).

7. *Determining a Quorum*

The Book of Church Order states that for a Session of three or more Ruling Elders, the pastor and two Ruling Elders shall constitute a quorum. When there is no pastor, if there are five or more Ruling Elders, three shall constitute a quorum; and if there are fewer than five, two shall make a quorum (§ 15-2). However, the Book of Church Order further states: "Any Session, by a majority of its members, may fix its own quorum, provided that it is not smaller than the quorum stated in this section" (§ 15-2). It might be wise for a Session (particularly as it gets larger) to set a quorum large enough to ensure that any action taken would be approved by a sufficient number of Elders, after full discussion and agreement. The number should not be set so high that a few absences would hamper the work of the Session; but on the other hand, it should not be set so low that it would permit a small minority to act for the Session. If a fairly large proportion of the Elders cannot be present, it is doubtful whether any decision on important issues should be attempted.

8. *Attendance*

Every Elder should be at every meeting of the Session unless he is "providentially hindered." Participation in the business of the Session is a matter not of choice but of covenant; and no officer should absent himself from stated meetings without sufficient cause. In any event, if by absenting himself an officer fails to perform his duties, the Session should practice the discipline of the Church as it is set forth in Section 107-8 of the Rules of Discipline. In order that accurate records may be kept, each Elder absenting himself from a stated meeting should be required to present his excuse to the court for its action.

9. Committees of the Session—General Structure

The number of committees will vary with the number of Elders, the size of the congregation, and the extent of the program. Thus, each Session will need to determine its specific needs in terms of committees. However, for our purposes here we will set forth five committees which grow out of the duties and responsibilities given in the Book of Church Order, particularly in Sections 11-4, 12-3, 12-5, and 15-6. These five committees will follow somewhat the suggestions of "A Suggested Guide for Administration in the Local Congregation," Chart A-3, page 11. Since these committees and their various duties will be dealt with in separate chapters, at this point our discussion will be limited to the general structure of committees.

Basically the Session will have three types of committees: permanent or working committees, temporary committees, and special Sessional committees. Let us look at them in turn.

The Permanent or Working Committees. These committees should be specified. For example, the Standard of Procedure should state: "The permanent (working) committees of the Session shall be . . ." Then three things must be determined about each committee. First, the membership of each committee must be set. That is, how many members will be needed to carry on the work of this particular committee? Second, it must be determined how these persons are to be selected. Will they be appointed by the Moderator, selected by the committee chairman, or selected by the Session? Will some be members by virtue of office in the church? Or will a combination of these possibilities be used? An example of a combination would be for the chairman to be elected by the Session and the other members to be appointed by the Moderator. Again, the Standard of Procedure might specify that the Session elect the chairman, that the church school superintendent serve by virtue of office, and that the rest of the committee be selected by the chairmen in conference together, with approval by the Session. Whatever system or combination of systems is used, the Standard should clearly specify the method to avoid confusion. Also, it would be wise to designate a vice-chairman, who should be an Elder— usually the first-named person after the committee chairman. It is usually wise for a Session to elect its committee chairmen. This relieves the pastor of an extra responsibility, prevents criticism of his choices, and precludes control by one person.

The third thing that must be determined about permanent committees is the specific duties of each particular committee. It is vitally important that each committee of the Session be given specific and designated responsibilities. Inefficiency and friction may arise in a Session when two or more committees are trying to do the same job, each feeling that it has sole responsibility. If the Standard of Procedure clearly states the duties of each committee, such a possibility is forestalled.

Temporary Committees. Temporary committees, such as a Building Committee, should be provided for so that some unusual responsibility or a temporary problem of large magnitude may be handled separately when it is not specifically covered in the duties of any permanent (working) committee. The Standard should specify who is empowered to create such committees and to appoint members to serve on them.

Special Sessional Committees. There are some matters committed to the Session as a Church court which cannot be assigned to a broadly based committee. Therefore, committees composed of *Elders only* should take care of such duties as reviewing the work of the Board of Deacons (see BCO, § 15-6(8)), dealing with matters of discipline (§ 101-2), and effecting the examination of church officers for ordination and installation (§ 29-2).

A committee should be fully structured. The Standard of Procedure should state the provisions for meetings, reports, records, absences, vacancies, and quorums of such committees. The work of the church is too important and vital to be left to chance. In order that work may be uniformly done and each phase of the Session's responsibility duly emphasized, each committee should have the same requirements.

It must be clearly understood that each committee operates under the review and control of the Session. All committees must report to the Session, which, as a Church court, is the governing body of the entire congregation (§ 14-5).

10. Committees of the Session—Personnel

The Session should take advantage of the various talents and abilities of individual members of the congregation and use them on committees of the Session. For example, most churches have competent men and women who can render a real service on the Committee on Strengthening the Church. A conscientious Session will diligently search for members with talents and will place them on committees through which those abilities can be put to work for the Kingdom. (For suggestions on the membership of committees, see the annual *Plan Book,* the Resource Guides, and "A Suggested Guide for Administration in the Local Congregation," Section E, pages 3-4.)

In training personnel for committee work, there are two things you can do to make your committees work more efficiently. First, you can offer a special training meeting for all committee chairmen. This should include instruction on planning a year's work, planning and spending a committee budget, and how to conduct a meeting. A second thing you can do is to offer a training period for committee members. This should include a general meeting of members of all committees, in which there is presented to them a synopsis of the total program of the church. This helps members to get their particular committee's work in perspective and see how it fits into the larger program of the church. Training and information on how to serve well on a committee should be included.

A meeting of members of all committees gives a fine opportunity for inspiration and fellowship. As they see how many are involved in the life and work of the church and as they see the possibilities for serving the Lord through their particular and unique talents, this meeting will be a source of continued encouragement throughout the year. Some Sessions have written into their Standard of Procedure provisions for such a program of training, to make sure that it is provided each year. Perhaps you will desire to do this, too.

11. Committees of the Session—Division of Duties

Let us turn for a moment to examine the duties and responsibilities of the Session and break them down into committee structure. Remember that no one specific form will fit every local church and its particular needs. However, on the basis of duties set forth in the Book of Church Order, we shall attempt to devise a committee organization that will meet the needs of the average church, enable the Elders to fulfill the duties of their office, and ensure that each phase of the Session's work is properly emphasized and adequately handled. Where leadership and manpower are available, any of the committees we shall suggest may be further divided; in the chapters dealing with the committees we shall indicate appropriate reasons for dividing a committee further. However, it may be well to sound a note of warning at this point. Many Sessions make a serious mistake in so dividing responsibility in order to "give every man a job," that sickness, business, or the irresponsibility of one man can completely inactivate some phase of the Session's work. (We know of one church with twelve Ruling Elders that had twelve committees!) Each committee should be of such size and have such responsibility that it will not only have a meaningful job to do but will also have the personnel to do it. It has been truly said that what is everybody's business is nobody's business! Therefore, each committee should have specific, designated jobs and responsibilities to perform and should be expected to fulfill its assignments.

Certain records are required to be kept by the Session (see §§ 8-7, 13-5, and 15-7, particularly). In order that the responsibility for these records may be under specific jurisdiction, these duties will be assigned to the Clerk. We shall discuss this office and its duties at length in a separate chapter. At this point we will concern ourselves with other duties, particularly those in Sections 11-4, 12-3, 12-5, and 15-6.

Because of the varied and extensive nature of the Session's responsibilities, it is difficult to establish a few committees that will adequately handle all the duties incumbent upon the Session. However, a close study of the duties indicates that the following committees will encompass most of the duties specified by the Book of Church Order as well as those which grow out of it by implication. The specific duties of the recommended committees will be spelled out in appropriate chapters as well as in the Standard of Procedure included in Appendix A. There are points at which a decision on where a duty goes is difficult to make, but as long as unspecified duties are assigned to some committee, the essential part has been taken care of. For our purposes, then, we will discuss organization for the work of the Church Session in terms of committees on Worship, Commitment, Witness, Service, and Strengthening the Church. (See the booklet, "A Suggested Guide for Administration in the Local Congregation," particularly page 11.)

Let us emphasize that these committees are not intended to be definitive; nor are we suggesting that this is the only division of responsibility. However, according to the various responsibilities of the Session as set forth in the Book of Church Order, this is a logical and comprehensive form of organization to enable a Session to guide the congregation in fulfilling its total mission. Let it also be emphasized that these committees can be combined in the very small church or further divided in the larger church. Precisely what committees are needed will be determined by the needs of each individual church in the light of the local situation. And even the local situation will change with time and circumstance. Your committee structure should be reviewed often to determine whether it is meeting the needs of the church. Change does not necessarily mean progress, but there can be no progress without change. Be vitally alive to and acutely aware of your local situation. Never let custom or tradition stand in the way of doing your job and doing it well.

12. Questions of Procedure

No Standard of Procedure will answer all the questions that will arise; nor will it meet all of the problems the Session will face. Therefore, for problems and questions not specifically covered by the Standard, some provision should be made whereby the Session can be guided in such a contingency. Of course, the Book of Church Order should always be consulted in these cases. Some such book as *Robert's Rules of Order Revised* would be a helpful guide to the Session on knotty problems of procedure. Such a guide should be specified in the Standard of Procedure as the final authority when unanswered questions of procedure arise.

13. Amendments

Since no Standard of Procedure is perfect and since circumstances and needs vary, every Standard should make some provision for change to meet new problems that arise. However, since your Standard will have been carved out of experience, the method of changing it should not be hasty. Allow time for prayer, thought, and diligent preparation before changes are made.

Relating the Work of the Board of Deacons and the Session

The responsibility for relating the work of the Board of Deacons and the Session rests with the Session alone. A special committee composed of Session members should be formed for this purpose, to serve as a liaison between the two bodies. Perhaps you will want to have a member of this committee meet with the Board of Deacons each month, to represent the Session in matters of policy. Such a representative can then make a more accurate report to the Session on the work of the Board, being intimately acquainted with it. You will of course want to consult with the chairman of the Board of Deacons on this matter. You probably will find him to be as eager as you are for the two groups to work harmoniously. The Session will also find it helpful to have someone interpret actions of the Session to the Deacons personally. An action in writing sometimes does not convey its true spirit and can lead to misunderstanding. Things oftentimes can be better said than written.

In overseeing the activities of the Board and its diligence to assigned duties, there are three primary duties for this committee.

1. Examining the Minutes

According to the Book of Church Order, the minutes of the Board of Deacons must be examined at least once every six months (§ 12-4). Here are some of the things you will look for in examining these minutes. First, it would be well to check the attendance of Deacons. If a particular Deacon is habitually absent, you should call this to the attention of the Session. We expect our officers to be diligent in attendance and we should require it. You will need to determine as nearly as possible whether the Deacons are faithfully overseeing those duties assigned to them by the Book of Church Order. Again, you will want to ascertain whether or not they are operating within and adhering to the policies established by the Session. This does not mean you are a sort of "gestapo," but that you are seeking to meet your responsibility to the Session, the Board, and the church.

2. Examining the Financial Records of the Board of Deacons

Since the financial records of the church are a part of the work of the Board, these, too, will be examined as a part of the minutes (§ 12-4). You will want to be sure that at least an annual audit is made of the books, that the congregation is being kept informed on the financial condition of the church, that money is disbursed to the objects to which it has been given, that each phase of the budget is receiving its allotted share, that adequate records are being kept, and that the financial affairs are being handled according to established policy. You should keep the Session informed of the financial condition of the church as well, for the Elders will need this information in the formulation of policy and program.

3. Making the Budget

The Book of Church Order states that "the regular budget and other important financial matters require the approval of the Session" (§ 12-3). Your special Sessional committee is responsible for working with the proper committee of the Board of Deacons in formulating the annual budget of the church. If the budget is formulated by a joint committee of Deacons and Elders, it is more likely to be acceptable. Although the Session must finally approve the budget, it is advisable to have it presented to a joint meeting of Elders and Deacons in order that they may discuss it fully, ask questions freely, and support it wholeheartedly. Also, since the congregation is expected to subscribe the budget, ordinarily it should be presented to them either for their information or for counsel. You will remember, of course, that if the salary of the minister is in any way affected, congregational approval is required and the consent of Presbytery must be secured in order to change the terms of the original call (§ 25-2 and § 26-3). In making the budget, each committee should be given opportunity to present a requested budget. Be careful to recommend that each phase of the work be allotted its rightful share of funds, that no part of the work of the Kingdom will suffer.

Other Responsibilities
of Special Sessional Committees

1. Working with Staff Members

While the work of the sexton is the responsibility of the Board of Deacons, the other members of the church personnel are the responsibility of the Session. This does not mean you "boss" the church staff, for the pastor is the chief administrator in the church offices. However, it does mean that someone has to be responsible for policies relating to working hours, salaries, working conditions, vacations, and so forth. Many church staffs suffer because there is no particular person or committee directly responsible for them. A special committee of the Session should function in this area. Let us look at some of the things this committee will want to consider.

Salaries. You should be diligent to see that salaries meet the standard of a living wage and reflect the training and experience of the employee. They should be re-evaluated each year and graded according to the cost of living. People who work for the church do not seek financial reward as a chief motive, but this should not be an excuse for the church to underpay its staff. Adequate remuneration is your way of expressing appreciation for services rendered. Also, do not let other needs take precedence over adequate salaries. Salaries along with benevolences are of vital importance.

Working Hours. Do not expect or require your church staff to work longer hours than anyone else. They usually do, but we should never grow to expect it. You should particularly be diligent to protect your pastor, not only from himself but from all the groups in the church and out of it that make demands on him. Many times he finds it difficult to say no. You can say it for him. While you will not want to attempt to regulate his work for him, you can caution groups and individuals about making too many demands on him and keep them conscious of the fact that certain limitations should be observed in their expectations. It should be clearly understood by staff members as well as officers what the working hours are and how much is expected of a particular staff person.

Working Conditions. While few people are conscious of it, church work is among the most difficult and demanding of all. Therefore you will want to be sure, in co-operation with the Property Committee of the Board, that office equipment, heating and cooling, decor, facilities, etc., are adequate. Don't require your church staff to work under conditions that you would not be willing to work under yourself! Any convenience and comfort you can provide for the minister, secretary, Director of Christian Education, or other staff person will result in increased efficiency. Money spent on proper equipment and facilities is an excellent investment.

Vacations. Members of a church staff are people, too! They need to get away from it all and leave their cares and worries behind, just as you do. Therefore, you will seek to ensure that all staff persons in your church have adequate vacation periods allotted to them. This is particularly true of the minister. The demands on him are tremendously heavy, and he cannot take an occasional weekend off to go "up country" as others can. If you err on vacations, let it be on the side of generosity!

Fringe Benefits. Of course you will want to protect your church staff by participating in the major medical and life insurance program of the Church for the minister and church employees. (Information may be had from the Board of Annuities and Relief.) In addition, you will want to be sure your minister and employees participate in the Ministers' and Employees' Annuity Fund program of our General Assembly. All staff persons should be adequately covered.

Defining the Job. Another important task you should undertake is the formulation of a "job analysis" for the various employees of the church. Often there is dissatisfaction with the administration of the church offices; and usually it can be traced to the fact that there is no clear understanding of what is to be done. For example, if you are going to hire a secretary, in cooperation with the minister you should draw up an analysis of the job you expect that secretary to do. Suppose again your church is hiring a Director of Christian Education. What do you expect of him? Who directs his work? How is he related to the Committee on Strengthening the Church? To other committees? These and many other questions must be answered. As an example of such a job analysis, we are including as Appendix B a sample of one used by a local church. This one happens to fit the needs of a particular church and is not necessarily a model. However, this Session has described what it expects of its Director of Christian Education. He knows and they know what is required, and everybody is better satisfied.

Even for part-time employees you should clearly state what you expect and precisely what the job is. For example, for a part-time choir director and organist, you will need to specify what you require. You will want to answer certain questions that will arise. A job analysis for the Director of Music and the organist will be found in Appendix D.

As you can see, your responsibilities are large in the field of the church staff. A well-organized church where at least the important things are done is the result of careful thought, planning, and concern. It will take some hard work, yes. But the dividends in increased efficiency, harmony, and understanding will more than repay you for the hours you spend.

2. *Exercising Discipline*

The Book of Church Order contains a section entitled "The Rules of Discipline." It states that "Discipline for correction . . . is committed to Presbyters to be exercised in Church courts" (§ 101-2). Therefore, this responsibility cannot be assigned to the Committee on Service, as a phase of pastoral care, nor to a broadly based Committee on Commitment. The exercise of discipline over church members, Ruling Elders, and Deacons, as directed in the Book of Church Order (§§ 101-2, 104-1, 104-2, 107-8), is one of several distinctive functions under jurisdiction of the Session.

The Session should have a special Sessional committee on discipline which can inform the Session in the event a process of discipline should be instituted. It is important that such a committee understand its function before problems arise, recognizing also that "discipline is to be exercised as under a dispensation of mercy and not of wrath" (§ 101-5).

In some states, Ruling Elders can hold communications as legally confidential when these have been revealed during processes of discipline by the Session. You should know whether this is true in the state in which you live. For further guidance in this and in other matters of discipline, the following books, available through your denominational book stores, are suggested:

> *Presbyterian Authority and Discipline,* by John Kennedy
> *The Right to Silence: Privileged Communication and the Pastor,* by William H. Tiemann

3. Relating to Other Church Courts

The Session is related not only to individual members and to the congregation, but also to the denomination as a whole. It will be your duty to examine the records of the General Assembly, Synod, and Presbytery for those matters that affect your congregation or Session and bring them to the attention of the proper group. In addition, you will nominate representatives to higher courts and will co-operate with those chosen in seeing that a report of their diligence is made to the Session as is required by the Book of Church Order.

Summary

To organize for the task may seem a difficult job—and it is! To set out all of the necessary rules of organization and to establish all of the policies and principles by which a Session will operate is a demanding task. But good things never just happen. They are the result of consecrated study and diligent planning. A limited number of important matters can be fully considered and adequately handled in the brief time that the Session has at a stated meeting. Only when each committee has done its work, investigated thoroughly, and prayed earnestly, and then presented a well-prepared report and recommendation, can the Session act faithfully and well.

IV

MR. MODERATOR

As the Moderator of the Church Session you, to a large degree, will shape the life, work, and program of your church. It is a heavy and demanding responsibility, but one you cannot escape. The Book of Church Order offers you no alternative. The question that faces you as Moderator, then, is how you can best do a difficult job. Even if you feel that you have no administrative abilities and even if other demands make this task seem burdensome, the nature of your office as pastor places it squarely on your shoulders. In this chapter our effort will be to help you fulfill this part of your task to the best of your abilities.

The fact that you are an ordained minister of the Presbyterian Church does not mean that you will automatically make a good Moderator. Although you may have many talents and abilities in the vocation that has chosen you, it does not necessarily mean that you will be a good leader of leaders. In your Session are men who are wise in the ways of the Lord and His Kingdom, men who are mature in the faith and experienced in many areas. To be able to command their respect and to lead the work of the Session competently will demand a tact and diplomacy, a consideration and thoughtfulness, that will tax your abilities to the limit. You will have to be a man among men, a Solomon among the wise, and an example among the devout!

To be a good Moderator will not be easy by any stretch of the imagination. In a very real sense, the Moderator influences the total life of the church through the Session. The kind of Session you have—the quality of performance and the faithfulness to the task—will largely be determined by you, the Moderator. Even with less than the best of leadership on his Session, a good Moderator can do an effective job in the local church. But with the very best of men, a Session will be hampered in its work by an ineffective Moderator.

With such a high responsibility, it is imperative that each Moderator fully understand the work of the Session and the nature of his responsibility. It is imperative that he have a thorough grasp of the extent of the duty that is his. Let us use this chapter, then, to think through some of the simple yet important items that will help a Moderator do his job more efficiently and effectively.

Conducting the Meetings of the Session

To a great extent the work of the Session will be determined by the quality of its stated meetings. The way in which discussion is conducted, the manner in which decisions are reached, the pattern for Sessional committees, the pride taken in duties well done, the importance placed on various jobs, create the whole atmosphere in which the Session moves and does its work. Do not take this responsibility lightly or do it poorly, for it is here that attitudes and opinions of your Elders are being formed. If the work you are doing is vital and important to you, you will convey this through the meeting. Unfortunately, if you do not feel this way about the things the Session does, this attitude is transmitted too. Let us look at some of the things that can be done to inspire the best attitude and to ensure that the noble task will be nobly done.

1. Making an Agenda

Every stated meeting should be planned in detail well in advance of the call to order. In consultation with the Clerk prior to the meeting, you will want to think through the order of business that is to come before the Session. If it is possible, the agenda for the meeting should be sent to each member of the Session in advance in order that all may know the items to be brought up and the order of business. In this way the Elders can intelligently prepare themselves to vote. Some Sessions even send out copies of recommendations to be presented by various committees, much as Presbyteries do. This policy is recommended. Elders who have had time to study and pray about important issues can then vote wisely.

What should an agenda include? It should include the order in which business is to be transacted, providing adequate time for new business that might demand the attention of the Session. A sample agenda might look something like this:

Agenda for Stated Meeting, The Session
First Presbyterian Church
Anywhere, U.S.A.

Time: 7:30 p.m.   Date: July 10, 19—

Call to order by Moderator and opening prayer
Period of worship
Declaration of quorum and recording of absences
Reading of minutes of past meeting
Letters and communications
Permanent (working) committee reports
    Worship
    Commitment
    Witness
    Service
    Strengthening the Church
Temporary committee reports
Special Sessional committee reports
Unfinished business
New business
Closing prayer and adjournment

Under each of these items, particularly the committee reports, specific things to come up should be listed in 1, 2, 3 order. Do not rely on someone else or on your memory to conduct the business of the Session. Write it down in its proper place.

2. Starting on Time

If a meeting is called for a specific time, it is not fair to those who are there to wait for others who may or may not come. You will develop the habit of punctuality among the Elders if they know that the meeting will start precisely at the time specified. Remember to be punctual yourself, for you are establishing the pattern. According to the Book of Church Order (§ 15-2 and §15-5), your Session cannot begin its meeting without you, the Moderator. If you are unavoidably detained, you should let them know at once and should explain your tardiness when you arrive.

3. *Opening with Prayer and Period of Worship*

The Book of Church Order requires that every court of the Church should open and close its meetings with prayer (§ 13-6). In addition, a brief opening period of worship sets the mood for the entire meeting and determines the atmosphere in which the business of the Session will be conducted. Through this exercise of devotion, the Word of God is brought to bear upon the business at hand and upon the hearts and minds of the Elders. The responsibility for these periods of worship should belong to your Worship Committee; they are an important part of every meeting and should not be ignored. Surely the Elders, who are responsible for the spiritual life of the congregation, would not presume to conduct their business without first opening their own hearts to the Holy Spirit. The example of Sessional devotion will carry far in your church.

4. *Recording of Absences*

While the Clerk of the Session is actually responsible for recording absences, it is your responsibility to be conscious of who is present and who is absent. Through the Clerk, it should be determined whether excuses have been presented to the court by those absent. The Moderator will want to be sure that excuses are carefully weighed and that appropriate action is taken. If an Elder is continually absent without excuse, it may become the responsibility of the Session to confer with him and if necessary to take action under its duties of discipline as set forth in Section 107-8 of the Book of Church Order.

As minister as well as Moderator, you will want to investigate the reasons for continued absences by an Elder and make every effort to impress upon him the significance of his calling and the seriousness of his failure to fulfill his covenant obligations. Simply to ignore such absences endangers the total work of the Session. Certainly an unhealthy attitude toward the office of Elder is generated when absences are passed over without investigation or action.

5. *Reading of the Minutes*

This is an important and necessary procedure and need not be burdensome. It is required that our minutes be read and approved. These are the permanent records of the Session and are subject to annual review by the Presbytery as required by Section 15-7 of the Book of Church Order. Since quite often a question arises as to the precise action taken by the Session at an earlier date, it is doubly important that all actions be recorded correctly in permanent form.

6. *Committee Reports*

The form of committee reports to the Session will be fully discussed in another chapter (see Chapter VI, "Making the Committees Work"). However, the faithfulness with which a committee chairman follows this form is going to depend in large part on the Moderator's insistence that reports be made in the proper manner. The Moderator would do well to familiarize himself thoroughly with the section dealing with the recommended form of reporting to the Session by committees. The Session is able to act intelligently and effectively on matters presented to it only if the matters are properly presented. For example, suppose the Committee on Worship reports, "We recommend that the Session employ a new organist." You can imagine the confusion. Whom will we get? How much will we pay? What will we require of this person? What qualifications will we insist on? A Session that has many other important items before it could spend a whole evening discussing such a problem and still not have a satisfactory solution. In instances such as this, the Moderator should refer such recommendations back to the committee for proper presentation. To a tremendous degree, the effectiveness of the Session hinges on the ability of the Moderator to require that reports be carefully prepared and that they recommend definite action.

7. *Old Business, Communications, and New Business*

Do not leave unfinished business hanging! Your Clerk is primarily responsible for bringing such items to the attention of the

Moderator, but ultimately the responsibility is yours. Communications and letters that demand the attention of the Session and that need answering should be taken care of as soon as possible. Nothing is more frustrating than to address an inquiry or request to some group and never get a reply! Be diligent to attend to the proper correspondence of the Session at each meeting. As for new business, give ample opportunity for it to be presented. However, if it presents a problem demanding time, thought, and study, do not attempt to handle it toward the end of a lengthy meeting, when minds are not as alert as usual. Either refer it to the proper committee for study and report, or appoint a temporary committee to report on the item at the next meeting, or simply docket it for first attention at the next meeting.

8. *Length of Meeting*

Do not stay in session all night! How often meetings last wearily on into the late hours! Nothing can do more to dampen the enthusiasm of Elders (and their families) toward the work of the Session than to have the meeting lengthen interminably. If the work of the Session cannot be adequately done within a reasonable time, then a special meeting should be called to handle the remainder of the business. People who have worked all day and must report for work the next morning simply cannot afford to stay up half the night. Neither their regular job nor the Session business gets adequate attention. However, if the Moderator keeps the meeting moving, holds irrelevant discussion to a minimum, hears only those reports that are properly presented, and handles debates adequately, there is no reason why a Session should stay up half the night to do its work. Do your work quickly and efficiently; if there are those who wish to "visit," let them do so after the meeting has been adjourned.

9. *Parliamentary Procedure*

As Moderator, it will be necessary for you to be familiar with the ordinary parliamentary procedures. Some guidance is offered in the back of the Book of Church Order. *Robert's Rules of Order Revised* will also be indispensable to your personal library. Since you will be called on many times in your ministry to rule on questions of procedure, you will need to do some real and earnest study on this subject. For moderating a Church Session a good rule of thumb is: the larger the number involved, the more strict the adherence to parliamentary procedure. If you have a small Session of eight or ten, the meeting may be run as informally as possible. But the larger it gets, the more you will have to stick to the rules.

10. Some Don'ts to Observe

(1) Don't ignore the ideas of others. You as the Moderator are to be an impartial chairman of a meeting; and it is not your responsibility to decide what is good and what is not good. Many Moderators get into trouble by trying to make decisions that rightfully belong to the entire Session.

(2) Don't insist on your own way. You may be absolutely right, but that isn't the way to win a debate. If you feel that you have a good idea or wish to enter into debate on a particular discussion, then you should relinquish the chair to the Vice-Moderator or the Clerk and take your turn in speaking to the question.

(3) Don't call brief meetings at odd times to act on questions that need the full consideration of the Session. It is better to be slow about a matter than to take a hasty, ill-advised action that you may regret later or may need to rescind.

(4) Don't minimize the work done by others. Give every person full credit for the work he has done, and give him proper time to report to the Session. People always do better work if they feel that what they are doing is important and appreciated.

11. Some Do's to Observe

(1) Do give everyone an opportunity to speak. Often the quiet fellow who doesn't have much to say has a real contribution to make to the Session if only he is given a chance to speak.

(2) Seek to keep an individual from dominating a discussion. If one man is pushing a particular pet idea and insists on speaking every other time, say something like, "Mr. Blank, since you

have already expressed your ideas to the Session, let's hear what someone else may have to say in regard to the motion."

(3) Hear both sides of a question. Sometimes the minority *can* be right even when you hold a different opinion.

(4) Be as fair as you can. If you begin to take sides on issues before the Session, your fellow Elders will soon lose confidence in your ability to serve as an impartial moderator of the meeting.

(5) Require recognition by the chair before allowing a member to speak. Several conversations at once are confusing and downright rude! Nothing is so disconcerting (or fruitless) as trying to speak to a question when several side conversations are going on. You may have to be firm at this point, but in the long run the Session will appreciate your firmness.

(6) Have orderliness in the meeting. The meeting can be too formal; but it can be so informal that it will effectively stop all work! A relaxed atmosphere with fairly strict requirements for discussion and debate is best.

(7) Be sure to read in Chapter VI the suggestions on conducting a meeting.

Working with Committee Chairmen

One of the most important parts of your responsibility as Moderator of the Session is your work with the chairmen of the various committees. You can have the very best Standard of Procedure and the most important work to do; but if your committees are not functioning properly, nothing will get done. Here, as minister and Moderator, you play an important "behind-the-scenes" role. It is your job to work with the chairmen of the committees, to encourage them, to inspire them, and— when necessary—to give them a gentle shove in the right direction! Yet, never must you give the feeling or impression that you are running the committee or doing its work or having all the ideas. Even if you are, you must be mature enough and secure enough to let others take the praise. Do you remember how Paul put it? He wrote, "I planted, Apollos watered, but God gave the growth. So neither he who plants nor he who waters is anything, but only God who gives the growth" (1 Corinthians 3:6-7).

Work closely with your committee chairmen. Talk over the work of the committees, share ideas, and make suggestions to them. Occasionally you may find it profitable to have a meeting with all of the chairmen together to talk about the work, the problems, the ideas, and the dreams of the men as they strive to fulfill the noble task. Many ministers have found that a regular practice of meeting with the chairmen of all committees is a wonderful stimulus to the work of the Kingdom. It may even become necessary from time to time to have a heart-to-heart talk with a particular chairman as you urge and encourage him to pursue diligently the area of responsibility assigned to him and his committee. Of course, it is extremely difficult to tell a man that he isn't doing his job and that he'd better get busy! It requires tact and diplomacy that would tax the most able. We cannot tell you how to do this since each case will vary; but starting with earnest prayer and sincere self-searching to see if you are at fault is a good beginning. As a further suggestion it would be helpful to get your committee chairmen off to a good start by offering them training for their duties. You might desire to follow the suggestions in Chapter III under subhead 10, "Committees of the Session—Personnel."

Working with the Board of Deacons

As the pastor of a church, you are not only Moderator of the Session; you are also an advisory member of the Board of Deacons (§ 12-4). And while you cannot vote on matters before the Board, they will look to you for wisdom, for advice, and for recommendations. Some ministers have the idea that their attendance at meetings of the Board of Deacons is not important, and they do not bother to attend. This not only violates the spirit of our government; it is unfair to the members of the Board. You are in a key position to know the church's total program, its needs, its goals, and its policies. Your advice will be of invaluable assistance to the Board as it formulates its program and does its work. Also, since you, as Moderator of the Session, stay in close touch with the total program of the church, it is imperative for your effective leadership for you to know what the Board is doing. On the other hand, it certainly does something to the spirit of a Board of Deacons if their pastor is not interested in their work or thinks it is not important enough to require his attendance. Use your wisdom, your knowledge, and your abilities to counsel and advise these men wisely as they grow in grace and in service to the Church. It is to be remembered that you have an important role in interpreting the Session and the Board of Deacons to each other.

Keeping Up with the Total Program

Unfortunately it is not always possible to assign to an individual or to a committee the responsibility for a job and get it done every time. Yet, initiative is destroyed if you give a job and do not expect it to be done. Somewhere in between is a happy medium that you must find. Is the Clerk keeping proper records? In what shape are the financial books of the church? What is going on in the Women of the Church? What is happening in the church school? Are visitors being welcomed? In a very real sense of the word, you are the overseer of the *total* work of the church. Like the captain of a ship, you must ultimately bear the responsibility for whatever happens. You must know what is going on in every area of the life of the congregation which you serve. You must know how the committees are functioning and how well the work is being done. Remember that the work of the Session—indeed, that of the entire church—will be as good as its Moderator and pastor; and its program, as effective as he is. It is not an easy job or a light responsibility, particularly for the man who takes his calling seriously; but, after all, you are not in the ministry because it is easy.

A General Summary

There is so much that could be said and perhaps should be. Yet, this at least points us in the right direction. The variety of duties, responsibilities, and tasks is simply amazing, for the noble calling is indeed a hard and exacting one. It demands diligence, faithfulness, unremitting attention, and a great deal of prayer.

V

THE CLERK OF THE SESSION: KEY MAN IN A KEY JOB

As the Clerk of your Session, you hold one of the most important jobs in your church. How well you do your job and how faithfully you perform your various duties will, to a large extent, determine how adequately the program of your church is carried on. Yours is an exacting job. There are many records that must be kept, most of them in more or less permanent form. There are letters to write, minutes to capture accurately on paper, programs to be kept up with, and a host of other duties and tasks to be performed. Since your duties are so varied, let us see if we can break them down into various phases to give you a clear picture of the total responsibility that falls upon you as Clerk.

Records to Be Kept

Aside from the minutes of the Session meetings, there are various records that should be taken care of. These records logically fall under your duties as Clerk.

1. The Active Roll

The Book of Church Order requires that the Session keep an active roll of its communing members (§ 8-7). This will include all members who have been baptized and have made their public profession of faith in Jesus Christ, including those who have come to your particular church by certificate of dismission from another church (§ 8-1), reaffirmation of faith (§ 8-2), or restoration from the inactive roll (§ 8-11). (See Section 7-1 for the definition of a communing member.)

2. *The Inactive Roll*

It is also required in Section 8-7 that the Church Session maintain a roll of its inactive members. Each year you will want to be sure that a careful check is made on the membership of the church and that those who have willfully refused to participate in its ordinances or who have not expressed a serious interest in the church be placed on this roll (§ 8-9). Also, anyone who has moved his residence and cannot participate shall be placed on this roll after one year, if he has neglected to have his membership transferred (§ 8-10). At the same time, those on this roll who have resumed participation in the life of the church should be placed once again on the active roll (§ 8-11).

3. *The Non-Communing Roll*

The third roll required to be kept by the Session is the non-communing roll. This consists of those children of believers who have not yet made their profession of faith in Christ and are not yet eligible for admission to the Lord's Table (§ 7-2 and § 8-7), but who have been baptized. Section 7-2 states that a child of believers who are communing members of a particular church is a member of the Church universal by right of birth. Such a child is entered on the non-communing roll in the particular church upon baptism (see § 8-7).

4. *Record of Significant Events*

In addition to these three rolls which record the relationship of individuals to the local church, other significant events in the lives of members should be carefully recorded. Therefore, the Book of Church Order requires that the Session keep an accurate record of dismissions, baptisms, deaths, and marriages (§ 15-8). As Clerk you will record any such events that have taken place since the last meeting and will ensure that the records affected are properly corrected.

5. *Other Items to Be Recorded*

While you are not responsible for the reading of the minutes of the Board of Deacons each six months (though it may be assigned to you by your Session), it is your duty to see that the report of such examination is recorded in the minutes of the Session semiannually. Also, you will want to be sure that the representatives to the courts of the Church report their diligence at meetings and that their report is recorded in the minutes. In addition, you will want to remind the Session of pending events, such as the election of officers if you have the limited term of service, or other actions that may be required at certain times by your Standard of Procedure.

6. A "Record Reminder"

A diligent Clerk might desire to have available at each stated meeting a "record reminder" to check over with the Session. It would simply be a list of things to remember. It might look like this:

1. Active Roll
   (1) Additions—by reception and by restoration from inactive roll.
   (2) Removals—by death, dismission to another church, transfer to inactive roll, or other action.

2. Inactive Roll
   (1) Additions—by transfer from the active roll.
   (2) Removals—by transfer, reactivation, death, or other means.

3. Non-Communing Roll
   (1) Additions—by baptism.
   (2) Removals—by transfer to active roll upon profession of faith or by transfer to another church.

4. Record of Significant Events
   (1) Marriages.
   (2) Representatives to Church courts—election of or report from.
   (3) Deaths or baptisms not otherwise reported.

5. Other Items

Do not leave these important responsibilities and items to chance. In the busy job of "clerking" at the meeting, you may forget some of these items if you do not have some way of reminding yourself, particularly if they do not recur at each meeting, as in the case of the report of representatives to courts.*

---

* For a fuller exposition, see *The Office of Clerk of Session* by Frank M. Beatty (Richmond, Virginia: John Knox Press, 1956).

Reports to Be Made

Not only are you responsible for the records of the Session; you are also responsible for the various reports it makes from time to time. One of these concerns extracts from the minutes of the Session. You are required to furnish such extracts when requested by your own Session or by a higher court (§ 13-5). Your minutes must be submitted to the Presbytery at least once a year for review and control (§ 15-7). Another report that your Session must make each year is the Annual Statistical Report, along with the Educational Report Form. These reports go to the Stated Clerk of your Presbytery. You will need help and information from others in making this report, particularly from the church treasurer and the Christian Education Committee; but the primary responsibility for the completion and return of this important annual report falls upon your shoulders.

Other Duties of the Clerk

In addition to these responsibilities, there are other duties that are yours by the nature of your office. It is through you that proposals made to Presbytery will pass. It is your job to issue certificates of transfer or dismission to other churches. You must see to it that the lawful injunctions of the higher courts are brought to the attention of the Session, particularly as reports and instructions from these higher courts come down to you. In examining your records annually, the Presbytery will ascertain whether the lawful injunctions of higher courts have been obeyed, so careful notation of this should be made. As you can see, there is much detail involved in your duties as Clerk of the Session. But all of them are important duties that should be carefully and diligently fulfilled to the very best of your ability. You will want to exercise care that you do your job well so that your Session will not be open to criticism from higher courts.

Recording the Minutes

One of the most important parts of your job as Clerk is to record accurately the transactions of your Session (§ 13-5). Let us examine some of the implications of this duty. Of course you must come prepared to write! Have an adequate supply of good paper and writing implements. As you prepare to record the minutes, there are several preliminaries to be observed. Let us look at some of them.

1. Statement of Time, Place, and Date of Meeting

Each set of minutes should begin by stating when the Session met, where it met, and at what time it convened. Undated minutes are of little help in attempting to determine the value a particular action might have or in furnishing extracts that will serve as "evidence to any ecclesiastical court and to every part of the Church" (§ 13-5). The Presbytery will be examining your records each year, and you will want them to be in proper form and order. For example, your minutes might begin:

> The Session of the First Presbyterian Church of Anywhere, U.S.A., met for its stated meeting of the month on July 10, 19—, at the church. The meeting was called to order by the Moderator, Mr. Jones, and opened with prayer by Mr. Smith.

Incidentally, be careful to note that the meeting was opened and closed with prayer, since this is required by the Book of Church Order in Section 13-6.

2. Recording of Attendance

It is important that the Clerk keep an accurate record of individual attendance for each meeting of the Session, both stated meetings and called meetings. It might be wise to have a standard mimeographed form which would include the information in Section 1 above, leaving blanks at the appropriate places. Then the name of each member of the Session could be listed, with a line in front of each name for an "X" to indicate presence and an "A" (or some other sign) to represent absence. This will save you considerable time as the meeting gets under way; at the same time it prevents you from forgetting anyone. When the Moderator calls for the recording of absences, you simply glance at your list and read off the names. Be sure to record excuses of those absent if they have been presented to you. If action against an officer becomes necessary for failure to fulfill his covenant obligation, your records will serve as a sound basis for such action.

3. Recording of Committee Reports

If a committee makes its reports to the Session properly, the report will be in written form, including the recommendations of the committee. It will be helpful to you and save considerable time at the meeting if the person making a motion to be voted on by the Session presents it to the Clerk in written form. With a little persistence and insistence, this can be accomplished. In this way you are assured of getting the motion as the maker intended it to be. Also, when committee reports are adopted by the Session for inclusion in the minutes, a great deal of time is saved if the Clerk requests committee chairmen to prepare these reports in written form in advance. There is nothing more time-consuming or deadening to a meeting than to halt all business while the Clerk laboriously records a report or a motion. Even when the report as a whole is not adopted for inclusion in the minutes, a good Clerk will keep a copy of such reports in a separate file for each committee, for easy reference. Most Sessions make the mistake of keeping inadequate records. Consequently, the plans, ideas, and actions of a few months past are forever lost. Sometimes a committee that has labored long and hard over a report has it come to naught simply because the fruits of their labor have been misplaced or lost through carelessness. A good Clerk with a wise use of effort and time can keep an accurate and up-to-date set of minutes and files that will prove of invaluable aid to the Session. This is your task.

4. Letters and Communications

Most letters and communications to the Session will come to you. It is your task to see that they are brought to the attention of the Moderator and that the Session takes the proper action. You should have a special folder or file in which correspondence to the Session is placed as it is received. Then, at the very first meeting of the Session, your folder is at hand and you are not forced to rely upon what may be a faulty memory. When presenting correspondence to the Session, you might say something like this:

> Mr. Moderator, we have a letter from the Council of Churches requesting the use of our church for Reformation Day services. I move that the request be answered in the affirmative and the details be referred to the Committee on Worship.

Or you might refer a letter in this way:

> Mr. Moderator, we have a request from a local charitable organization asking that they be included in our benevolence program. I move that this matter be referred to the Session's Committee on Commitment and that they, in conjunction with the Budget Committee of the Board of Deacons, present a recommendation to the Session; further, that the Clerk be instructed to advise this group that their request is under consideration.

In this manner requests, information, etc., coming to the Session are channeled by you to the proper committees for action; and the Session does not waste valuable time discussing issues which, at the moment, might be debatable.

5. *Unfinished Business or Old Business*

It is your responsibility to see that unfinished business, tabled motions, etc., are not left hanging, but are properly brought to the attention of the Session. At each meeting where unfinished business, etc., is left, you would do well to make a note to yourself and perhaps include it in your folder of correspondence; otherwise, a month later when the Session meets again, you may have completely forgotten the matter.

6. *Reading and Approving Minutes*

At each stated meeting of the Session, you will want to read the minutes of the last stated meeting as well as minutes of any called meetings prior to the present meeting. Do not read them hastily or slur your words. You are responsible for these minutes; and if you have accidentally recorded something erroneously, you will want to have it corrected. Read in a strong, clear voice so that all can hear and understand.

In order that the records may show that they have been properly read and approved, notation should be made on each set of minutes. First, the minutes should be signed by you at the bottom of the last page, on the right-hand side. Then, secondly, over on the left-hand side of the page, a notation similar to this should be made:

Minutes read and approved: _____
                                                                   (Date)

Signed: _____
                              Moderator of the Session

When this is done, those who examine your records are assured that the minutes have been properly approved and that the records are attested correct as shown.

7. *Keeping Minutes as Permanent Records*

The records that you have been elected to keep are to be permanent records of the Church Session. Much of the history and life of the church are going to be recorded therein. Therefore, you will want to do several things about your minutes. First, the records should be kept neatly. It is best to have the minutes typed. If this is not possible, be sure they are written in a clear, legible hand. As your work becomes a matter of record and history, you want the minutes to be something that will be a credit to you and the Elders with whom you serve. Second, keep them in some permanent form. A loose-leaf binder is not satisfactory because pages can get torn out too easily. There are numerous permanent binders available at your Presbyterian Book Store for nominal cost. Pick the one that best suits your needs. Third, keep the minutes in a safe place. They should not be left where anyone can get to them or read them. They are *not* public property; and matters may be recorded therein that should not be common to all. Also, you will want to put them in a place where insects, pests, dampness, etc., cannot damage them. If possible, records should be placed where fire cannot destroy them.

The Clerk as Parliamentarian

Another important duty of the Clerk at any meeting of the Session is to assist the Moderator by acting as parliamentarian. This means that you need to familiarize yourself thoroughly with the standard orders of procedure. So much so, in fact, that without having to stop and look it up, you will be able to answer almost any question that may arise. The demands on you at this point wll depend on the size of the Session. The smaller the Session, the less strict it will be; and the larger it gets, the more exact the parliamentary processes should be. In any event, you should be prepared if and when the need arises. You will find some help in a section of the back of the Book of Church Order entitled "Rules of Parliamentary Order." Although these rules are for the General Assembly meetings and are not binding on the Session, you are free to adopt them if you desire. A helpful examination of these rules and procedures and an interpretation of various parliamentary actions will be found 'in the appendix of the book *Presbyterian Polity and Procedures,* by P. J. Garrison, Jr. This book is now out of print, but there may be a copy at your church. In addition, you should study some such book as *Robert's Rules of Order Revised.* One point to remember is that the Moderator is the one who must rule on a point of procedure. You are simply to advise and counsel him upon his request. However, it may be necessary on occasion to remind him of a point of order. For example, if someone starts to make a motion when another motion is already before the Session, you might say, "Mr. Moderator, a point of order. There is already a motion before the house." On this matter of parliamentary procedure, you can render a real and valuable service to the Moderator and the Session. It will depend on how well you are prepared. Do not take this part of your responsibility lightly, as you may be able to save the Session much valuable time and keep it out of verbal and procedural log-jams.

Notifying Members of Meetings

Sometimes the record of attendance of Elders at meetings of the Session is somewhat less than satisfactory. At this point the

Clerk can render a valuable service to all by being diligent to remind the members of meetings, both stated and called. Sometimes it is said, "They know that the meeting is on that day every month and should not need to be reminded." Ideally, that is perfectly true, and for many people it is sufficient. Practically, it doesn't always work out that way! Even the most devoted of Elders is subject to lapses of memory and occasionally needs to be reminded of meetings.

The Clerk has several methods at his disposal for notifying members of meetings. If the Session is sufficiently small, he may personally call each member. Again, he can notify the committee chairmen; and they in turn can notify the members of their committees. A letter or postcard will often do the job. Some Clerks mimeograph a supply of postal cards in addressed sets with blanks for the date, time, and place. It is then a simple matter each time to fill in the blanks quickly and drop the cards in the mail. Also, it would be wise to include an announcement in the Sunday bulletin prior to the meeting. It not only serves as a further reminder to the Elders, but also lets the congregation know that the Session is diligently pursuing its business. Don't leave this announcement to the church office staff to remember. It's *your* job! Write out what you want put in, and leave it with the person who prepares the bulletin.

Correspondence of the Session

Usually it will be your job to conduct the correspondence of the Session. Any time you write a letter from the Session, you are doing public relations work for the church. Those to whom you write are going to judge your church and your Session by that letter. Since good public relations never hurt anyone, you will want your letters to reflect neatness, good taste, courtesy, and correctness in spelling, grammar, and punctuation. Remember that often it is not so much what you say as how you say it. Also, you should take care of necessary correspondence as soon as possible. It is disconcerting to direct a question or inquiry to some group and be forever in getting a reply. The ordinary process of getting the letter answered by the Session takes enough time without the Clerk's compounding the felony!

A further duty that every competent Clerk will want to take upon himself is to notify persons or committees of actions or policies that may affect them. Even when a committee chairman has been at the meeting where his committee was instructed to do a particular thing, it is helpful to his committee to have the exact wording of the instructions from the Clerk. Also, actions and policies that affect the Board of Deacons should especially be transmitted to them immediately as a matter of courtesy, since they have no other way of knowing what has taken place. Misunderstandings are often avoided in this manner.

The Place of Meeting

It is important that the place of meeting be prepared before the business of the Session begins. The Clerk should arrive sufficiently early (or make prior arrangements) to arrange tables, comfortable chairs, ashtrays, etc., so that as the Elders arrive, they can take their places and the meeting can begin on time. Be sure there are sufficient chairs for latecomers so that the business will not be disturbed as someone noisily drags in a chair. You will also make sure that the room is properly ventilated and well heated or cooled, as the need may be. A room too hot can make the Elders so drowsy as to ruin the best meeting. This is a small detail, but a very important one.

A Brief Summary

By this time you are probably overwhelmed by the extent of your duties and responsibilities! It is true that as Clerk you have a very large responsibility in your church. Your job is a demanding one, and its tasks should not be assumed lightly. To do the job well will take constant vigilance and continued application of your very best. In a large measure you can tremendously help or seriously hinder the work of your Session and your church by the manner in which you do your job. It is indeed a noble task. It is one that asks much of you, but which—at the same time—is as rewarding as any you will have the privilege of doing.

VI

MAKING THE COMMITTEES WORK

This chapter is designed primarily for those who will serve as chairmen of the various committees of the Session. While responsibilities for each committee will vary, there are some general principles for operating a committee that will be applicable to all. The effectiveness of a committee depends in the final analysis on the chairman of that committee. What are his duties, his particular responsibilities? How does one go about accomplishing these and getting the work done? It is with such questions that we will now deal.

Smaller Committees in General

Since in all probability your committee will be relatively small, many of the duties and responsibilities that would be carried out by others in a larger committee will fall on your shoulders as chairman. Let us look at some of these duties.

1. Notifying Members of Meetings

Since you probably will not have a regular secretary, ordinarily the chairman should call the meetings, set the time, date, and place, and be responsible for notifying the members. You probably will not need a regular date for meetings. You will need to meet more often at some times than at others; the nature of your committee responsibility will determine the frequency of your meetings. However, every committee should meet briefly at least once a month to review its work and to prepare its report to the Session, even if the report merely states,

"The Blank Committee met on such and such a date. There is no report to be made to the Session at this time." *Always* notify your committee members immediately prior to the meeting date and remind them of it. You will have better attendance that way.

2. *Minutes of the Meeting*

You may want to appoint one of the committee members to serve permanently as secretary; or you may prefer to appoint someone at each meeting. You may desire to keep the minutes yourself. In any event, always have pen and paper available. The minutes should be kept in a neat and orderly fashion. Ordinarily a copy should be given to the Clerk of the Session for use by the elected officers or for filing. Your records should be kept in such a form that those who succeed you can reap the fruits of your labor and experience and can readily discover what has been done in the past.

3. *Formality of Meetings*

"The smaller the group, the more informal the procedure" is a good principle to follow. You can wreck the enthusiasm and spontaneous contributions of an effective small committee by bogging it down with parliamentary rules. Of course, in a large committee rules are more necessary; but in a smaller committee they may interfere with fruitful discussion.

4. *Getting Off to a Good Start*

Always open and close your meetings with prayer. This is not an empty ritual we go through, but a profound opening of the mind and soul to the will of Him whom we are called to serve. It is always appropriate to have a Scripture reading or a brief period of worship as you get the meeting under way. The more receptive we are to God as we begin our work, the more effective our work will be.

5. *Beginning and Ending the Meetings*

Begin your meetings on time. If a member is detained, it is

not fair to the others to make them wait for his arrival. You can briefly fill him in when he comes. And then, stop within a reasonable time. It is better to have a second meeting than to attempt to do the work of the church when you are tired and worn out and when members are in a hurry to get home. It is not fair to the committee members—or to the work to which you are assigned—to do it without proper consideration and study.

6. Appointing Subcommittees

If your duties are many and varied, it may be necessary to appoint subcommittees either permanently or from time to time as the need arises. For example, if you are chairman of the Committee on Strengthening the Church, you will probably want a Home and Family Nurture Subcommittee as a permanent part of your committee. However, one danger you will want to avoid is too much division of duty. The smaller the committee, the more it should operate as a committee of the whole on matters for which it is responsible. Don't feel that you have to give everyone a job.

Doing the Work of the Committee

It is important that every committee fully understand the responsibilities that have been assigned to it. Therefore, as chairman it is your responsibility to lead the group in a thorough examination of its task. If your Session has a Standard of Procedure, the duties of your committee will be spelled out for you in considerable detail. It is imperative that your group spend much time in the first few meetings getting duties and responsibilities firmly fixed in mind. In the event your Session does not have any sort of Standard to list your duties, your committee will need to spend some time thinking through just what is expected of you and what your tasks are.

As your committee examines its assignment, there are some questions that it will want to ask itself. Let us look at some of these basic questions.

1. Pinpointing the Job

What is your job? You may want to write down or make notes

for the group on what its specific task is. If you are a member of the Worship Committee, for example, it is not enough to say simply that your job is to take care of the worship of the church. Your group should think through what this involves and be specific about what it means to lead the church in worship. In this case, you would want to think through such things as music, instruments, director of choirs, supply pastors, special services, etc.

2. Benefiting from Past Experiences

How has this work been done in the past? This is the next question your committee will want to ask itself. Don't be too hasty to discard old methods, for they usually arise out of experience. On the other hand, don't feel bound to a particular thing simply because it has always been done that way.

3. Seeking New Ideas

What are the possible ways of doing the job? Are there different ways, new ways, better ways of doing a job than those that have been used in the past? Every possibility should be thoroughly examined and critically scrutinized from every conceivable angle.

4. Finding the Best Way

Having described the problem, how it has been solved in the past, and how it may be done differently, your committee must now decide what is the *best* way to do the job. Sometimes the church may have failed to make progress or to keep pace with the rapidly changing demands of the times in which we live. The reason is that we have failed to examine critically ourselves and our customary ways of acting and have not been zealous to inquire whether a better way can be found. If each committee will be diligent to follow these steps and choose the best way of doing a particular job, the work of the Session will move forward and the quality of our service will improve.

5. Translating Ideas Into Action

Having made some decisions about duties and ways of performing them, the committee must now decide how to go about translating ideas into action. This will come in terms of appointing individuals or subcommittees to begin a task; or it will come in the form of recommendations to the Session. Ideas are of no avail unless we turn them into reality by hard work. As Jesus once put it, "We must work the works of him who sent me, while it is day; night comes, when no one can work" (John 9:4).

6. Following Up on Assignments

When a subcommittee or an individual is assigned some particular task or responsibility, the chairman should always ask for a report at the next meeting. When a person has been assigned a task and carries it out, appreciation and interest should be shown by having him report his actions to the committee. By the same token, requiring a report to the group serves as a control to assure the committee that its work is being done.

Using the Yearly Plan Book

Each year, under the auspices of the Inter-Agency Committee, our denomination produces a yearly plan book, entitled *Presbyterian Plan Book*. This will be one of the most useful tools your committee can have. One of the most important things it will contain is a Resource Guide for each of the four major areas of Commitment, Witness, Service, and Strengthening the Church. In addition, it will contain the names and addresses of the various agencies of our Church, the Hymns of the Month, the Church calendar for the year, monthly activities and emphases, and much other useful information. As you plan your program for each month, and as you make your general plans for the year, this will be an indispensable piece of material. These books are ready for distribution in the early fall for the following year, and you may order them from your Presbyterian Book Store. Each member of your committee should have a copy of the *Plan Book,* and you will want to refer to it regularly as your committee makes its plans.

Reporting to the Session

Each committee should make a full report of its activities to the Session each month. If recommendations are to be presented or authorization is to be sought, these should be presented clearly, simply, and intelligently. Since a failure to report properly to the Session results in a waste of time, let us look at some of the general principles that should guide a chairman in making his report.

1. *Avoid Boring the Brethren*

Do not read the minutes of your committee meeting. The Session has assigned to your committee a particular task. They are not so interested in how and when and where you went about doing it, but more in whether you *did* it. A brief summary of the meeting is entirely in order, but it should bring out only the pertinent points and issues involved. Nothing can so capably throw cold water on a meeting of the Session as a long recital of the minutes of some committee. Your minutes should be available for quick reference in the case of questions, but do not inflict them upon your fellow Elders without good cause!

2. *Reporting Your Actions*

As we stated above, the Session *is* interested in what you have done, so *do* report your actions! They want to know whether your committee is doing its job and what has been accomplished. If particular assignments have been made to your group, the Session will want to know the outcome. For example, suppose your group is the Committee on Witness. Your report might read something like this:

> The Committee on Witness met once this past month. Our Andrew Club continues to visit each Wednesday and made 35 calls on prospective members since our last report. We wish to report that according to the Session's authorization, a registration desk has been placed in the Narthex; and the Women of the Church have agreed to supply a hostess each week to greet our visitors and have them sign the registration book. Work planned for the immediate future includes a survey of

the Northwood district. We are also investigating the use of a listing service that provides the names of new residents in our neighborhood. Future plans include our annual week of special evangelistic services, on which work has already begun in cooperation with the Committee on Worship.

A report such as this informs the Session of your diligence, of what has been done, and of what you plan to do. No time is wasted, and the pertinent information is conveyed to the Session.

3. Making Recommendations to the Session

Misunderstandings start when recommendations to the Session are improperly made. Most recommendations require study, planning, and investigation before they are presented to the Session. Adequate decisions cannot be made unless the facts and figures are in hand to serve as a basis upon which decisions are reached. When a committee makes a recommendation to the Session on which it desires the Session to act, the recommendation should not only grow out of study and planning; it should be so precisely formulated by the committee that its passage will assure the accomplishment of it. The committee should prepare the recommendation beforehand and should come to the Session with a motion ready to present.

Let us again take the Committee on Witness to illustrate this point. Suppose a method for getting the names of new residents in the community is needed. Certain groundwork must be done by the committee. What methods are available? What expense is involved? Which plan is the most workable? These and other questions are handled in committee. When the committee has reached a decision after thorough investigation, its report and recommendation to the Session might read:

> The Committee on Witness has investigated the various methods of obtaining the names of new residents in the community and has concluded that a professional service best meets our needs. Therefore, we recommend that the Session authorize the Committee on Witness to enter into a six-month agreement with the Newcomer Service, Inc., at the rate of $15 per month, such funds to be charged against the budget of the Committee on Witness.

The Session does not spend fruitless time discussing a question on which nobody has specific information. It is now simply a matter of acting on a clear-cut recommendation that leaves no doubt about what is needed. If every committee would investigate the necessary facts of a matter and clearly formulate the recommendation to effect the proper action, much time would be saved and the Session could act on fact and not on fancy.

4. The Need for Written Reports and Recommendations

The chairman of each committee should present his report to the Session in written form. This serves several functions. First, it keeps reports from being too long and repetitious. Second, it makes them accurate. Third, it prevents the chairman from forgetting something that might be omitted in an oral report. Fourth, it can then be presented to the Clerk for inclusion in the minutes if so desired. It is to be noted that the form of report suggested under Section 2 above is short, informative, and to the point.

It is particularly desirable that recommendations for action to the Session be written out. It is time-consuming to have to stop while the Clerk writes down a long or involved motion. If the report is prepared by the committee in advance and presented to the Clerk in written form, this ensures several things. First, as mentioned, time is saved. Second, the report is recorded as the committee intended for it to be. Third, the desired action is either properly accomplished or authorized. And fourth, when the committee formulates its recommendation, the process serves to clarify its own thinking.

Some General Items to Remember

As chairman of an important committee of the Session, you will want to remember or be conscious of several general items as you work with your committee.

1. Why You Are Meeting

Always know why you are meeting. If you have no reason to

meet, don't! The average church member has enough meetings to attend without our burdening him unnecessarily. If you do have some reason to meet, have the need or problem clearly worked out to present to the committee.

2. *Giving Every Member a Chance*

You are not the boss of the meeting; you merely chair it. Don't insist on your way or your ideas. By the same token, do not let another individual dominate the meeting. The atmosphere should be such that all will feel free to enter into discussion and participate in the decisions of the committee.

3. *Giving Credit Where Credit Is Due*

We expect a lot out of our volunteer workers in the church, and rightly so. Our error is in not expressing proper appreciation. We do not work because we will be thanked, but appreciation does make us feel better about it! Any time you can show recognition, approval, appreciation, or simply give a slap on the back, do it! Next time you will have a more willing worker. Look for opportunities to express thanks, and you will find more of them.

4. *Keeping Your Committee on the Right Track*

Committees sometimes spend more time "visiting" and engaging in friendly talk than they do on the business at hand. The atmosphere of a small committee should be friendly and relaxed; but as chairman, it is your duty to see that the job is done within a reasonable time. Keep the meeting moving and on the business at hand. You can always bring the conversation back to the issue by reminding the group of what you have been discussing.

5. *Keeping the Issues Clear*

As chairman it is your duty to clarify issues. You will do this by making occasional summaries of what has been said on a particular topic, until all possibilities have been clearly presented. After a final summary, your group is ready to vote on the question at hand and do it intelligently.

Your Committee and Its Budget

Each committee ordinarily has a specific amount designated in the budget for its particular work. Unless authorized by the Session or congregation, you will be expected to stay reasonably within this budget. Therefore, your committee will want to plan its work well and thoroughly in order to operate within your financial means. Over the year you will probably discover items that should have been included in the budget or will need to be included in the next year's budget. Be sure to make notes of these items so that when information is requested of your committee by the Budget Committee, you can present a realistic budget proposal for the coming year.

It is essential to keep account of your expenditures so that you will always know where you stand in relationship to your budget; and as nearly as possible, you will want to plan your program sufficiently far in advance to ensure that the most important part of your responsibilities is adequately done. For example, if your committee is the Committee on Worship, do not spend all of your money on special services during the first part of the year and come up in August with no funds to pay a supply pastor when your minister is on vacation!

Working with the Moderator of the Session

You will want to work closely with the pastor and keep him informed of the committee's activities and plans. From time to time you may wish to invite him to sit in with your committee. Since he is intimately familiar with the over-all work of the church, he is in a valuable spot to advise and counsel you. Take advantage of his knowledge and ability, but don't depend on him to do your job!

Your year as chairman of a committee of your Session can be a year of real contribution and service for you and your fellow committee members. It will take faithfulness and perseverance; but the crown for which you strive is worthy of the race. A large responsibility rests upon your shoulders; and it is your high duty to fulfill it to the very best of your ability. Your Session, your church, your Lord—all are counting on you.

VII

THE COMMITTEE ON WORSHIP

Every committee of the Session plays an important and necessary role in the life of the local church. Through your efforts many things can be done to improve the experience of worship in your church.

The general responsibilities of your committee will include oversight of the services of worship in the local congregation; the administration of the sacraments; and special services, such as for Holy Week or for funerals and weddings. In addition, you will be responsible for the ministry of music in your congregation, for pulpit supply in the absence of the minister, and for anything else that relates to the continuing worship of your congregation.

Planning the Regular Services

There are many things you can do to make the regular services of worship in your church more reverent and beautiful. In conjunction with the Property Committee of the Board of Deacons, you will, of course, be sure that the sanctuary is "spic and span," that hymnbooks are in good condition, that pew racks do not have an accumulation of old materials, and so on. However, there are other specific items that properly call for your attention.

1. Sanctuary Appointments

There are some traditional sanctuary appointments you can use in your church which not only increase its beauty but also serve as silent reminders of the God who makes known His love in Jesus Christ. For example, a cross appropriately located reminds the worshiping congregation of what Christ has done for us on Calvary. The fact that the cross is empty, having no figure upon it, testifies to our *risen* Lord who has triumphed over the worst that sin could do. Some churches use pulpit falls and Bible markers in different colors to emphasize the seasons of the Church year. For example, the Trinity season has the color green, and the pulpit fall could have a trefoil and triangle symbolizing the Holy Trinity.

In worship the primary fact is what God does for us as the Word of God is read and preached. We worship as we receive God's gift of grace and respond in grateful obedience. Get one or more good books on worship and let your committee study them, then keep them available in your church library. (From among the many books available, the following are suggested: *Resources for Worship,* by Clarice Bowman; *Our Christian Symbols,* by Friedrich Rest; *Christian Symbolism in the Evangelical Churches,* by Thomas A. Stafford; *Within the Chancel,* by Thomas A. Stafford; *Symbolism in Liturgical Art,* by LeRoy H. Appleton and Stephen Bridges. These may be ordered through your denominational book stores.)

2. Choir Robes

If your choir is not robed, you may desire to work toward this. Well-styled, well-fitted robes of fine material should be used. You can encourage the choir members to see that the robes are kept clean and in good repair. It will help if there is good and adequate storage for them during the week to protect them. Avoid colors that attract too much attention to themselves. If you decide on stoles for the choir in the liturgical colors, you will want a neutral color for the robes that will go well with the green, purple, white, or red colors to be used in the stoles.

3. Flowers

Flowers that are well arranged can be very attractive, but avoid displaying them too prominently. We come to worship

God, not nature! At times during the year, yard flowers from members can be used. It may be wise, however, to select some person who is adept at arrangement to be available to help anyone who provides yard flowers. Many churches place a flower calendar in some convenient location to permit members of the church to sign up for a date when they will give flowers. For special dates such as Easter and Christmas, however, perhaps the church should give the flowers. You will want to include this item in your committee budget.

4. Order of Service

While the Committee on Service is responsible for producing the Sunday bulletin, you will want to consult with the minister about the order of worship as well as to work with the committee producing the bulletin. A poorly ordered service or badly printed bulletin can detract from the spirit of worship in the congregation.

The Administration of the Sacraments

A memorable experience in the life of the church is the administration of either of the two sacraments.

1. Baptism

Although you will have little responsibility for the actual administration of the sacrament of baptism, there are still several things you can do to help make it a meaningful service. In cooperation with the minister, you will want to see that the parents presenting children have an opportunity to learn of the significance of baptism and of the vows they will take. After the service, provide them with one of the baptism certificates available from your Presbyterian Book Store. Be sure that fresh water is in the baptismal font each Sunday. Also, since this is a great act of the church in which the congregation assumes a responsibility with the parents, we think it appropriate for one or more members of the Session to stand beside the minister, representing the congregation, during this solemn act. You will want to be sure that the presenting members are conveniently seated near the front and that they are instructed on what to do afterward. For example, if the child is to be taken to the nursery, be certain that the parents know where it is and how to get there quietly. If there are to be other members of the family present, you will want to reserve seats for them near the front where they can see and hear well. Such acts of thoughtfulness mean much to the family. It is to be remembered that the Session is to "instruct parents who are communicants to present their children for Baptism" (§ 15-6 (3)). Your committee should be diligent to fulfill this duty.

2. The Lord's Supper

When we turn to the serving of the Lord's Supper, there is more you can do to make this a memorable event. Let's look at some of the things you will want to consider.

Preparation of the Elements. This is a high and sacred task and may be assigned to the Women of the Church. They will see that it is properly done by persons given this responsibility. Your committee will notify them of special occasions for the celebration of the Lord's Supper.

The Vessels of Communion. If there is any "luxury" in the church, it should find expression in the communion vessels. Nothing is so distracting or harmful to a feeling of sacredness as to have cheap or stained communion vessels. Be sure that they are well cleaned and highly polished. The cloth on the table should be of fine white linen and beautifully pressed. Your own feeling of reverence will be impressively conveyed to the worshipers through the communion appointments.

After each use, the glasses and the communion trays will of course be cleaned and put away carefully by the persons responsible for their care.

Serving the Elements. A reverently served Lord's Supper doesn't happen by accident; it takes planning and rehearsal. Sit down with your minister and work out where each serving Elder should sit, where he should stand, and so on. (For instance, walking down the aisle naturally is quieter and less conspicuous than the attempt to keep in step.) When the details are all worked out, get your Session together and rehearse the service numerous times. When every man knows when to do what, the mechanics of serving will add to rather than detract from the service.

Serving the Sick and Shut-ins. Although the Lord's Supper is not a private act, but a public one of the Church, at *least* once a year you will want to provide communion for the sick and shut-ins of your congregation. We recommend World-Wide Communion Sunday in October as an appropriate occasion for doing this. Arrangements with the communicants should be made in advance, and several Elders should accompany the minister. You will find this an enriching experience, both for you and for the persons served.

Planning Special Services

At times during the year your committee may sponsor certain special services. For example, during Holy Week you may want special services, or surely a communion service for Maundy Thursday. You may have services at other times during the year, as at Thanksgiving, Christmas, and New Year's Eve. Also, some special services may be planned in co-operation with the Committee on Witness. Meet with your minister and look over the calendar of the Church year, then decide together what special services will be most helpful and plan them well in advance.

Two types of special services to which you will want to give particular attention are weddings and funerals. Recent concern about funerals and the discussion of the subject in numerous books and articles makes it appropriate for your committee to think through the meaning and significance of the funeral. Perhaps you will want to prepare for your particular congregation a booklet that will offer suggestions and help to a family when death comes. This would include a suggested procedure for the funeral, an order of worship, suggested music that is appropriate, and other details that would help the family through a difficult time as they make hard decisions. Also, it would be appropriate for your committee to develop a similar manual or booklet for the person getting married. It should include limitations on the use of the sanctuary, suggestions for decoration that are in keeping with our Reformed concept of worship, appropriate music, and other details that will be helpful to those planning a wedding. You might appoint a special subcommittee to do study on these two items and to draw up booklets for approval by the Session. Such helps will be deeply appreciated by those who use them, and you will be developing among your people a meaningful concept of worship that reaches into all of life, including the happy and the sad.

Supplying the Regular Ministry of the Word

It will be helpful to your congregation (and perhaps to your Presbytery) to develop Elders who are capable of conducting worship services. You can help prepare these men by using them when your own minister is absent or on other special occasions, such as Laymen's Sunday. Also, you can use a layman from time to time in the evening or midweek service.

You will be responsible for seeing that the pulpit of your church is filled when your minister is absent for reasons of sickness, church affairs, or vacation. While you may be able to use your own men, it may also be necessary to bring in guest ministers from time to time. Contact the Chairman of the Commission on the Minister and His Work for a list of the men who are approved and available for pulpit supply in your Presbytery. It is not your minister's duty to find a pulpit supply when he is absent; it is yours. Appoint a capable Elder to serve as host for the guest on that morning, to go over the service with him beforehand, perhaps taking part in it, and to introduce the visitor to your congregation. Take care of the details!

The Ministry of Music

Part of your responsibility will be working with the choir, its director, and the organist. Since these are really different responsibilities, let us look at them separately.

1. The Choir

As we have noted, you may desire to help the choir by providing robes for the members. Also, you will work with the choir and its director for special services of music, such as an Easter cantata. You should work with them in providing adequate rehearsal space—and comforts, too. The choir director alone should not be responsible for recruiting members. Your committee will want to co-operate with the director and the choir in this job. Necessary rules for the choir should come through your committee.

2. The Director

You will want to provide for the purchase of choir music by allocating in your committee budget an amount to be dispensed at the request of the director. Of course, you should require that a catalogued library of the church music be kept up to date. In co-operation with the Committee on Commitment, you should prepare a job analysis for the director (see Appendix D). He needs to know what you expect of him, and you also need to have this clearly in mind. The director should be responsible to you for his over-all program of music. If there is trouble or difficulty (someone has said the choir can be the devil's doorway into the church!), it is your responsibility—not the minister's—to deal with it.

3. The Organist

Here again you will need to formulate a job analysis in co-operation with the Committee on Commitment of your Session (see Appendix D). All concerned are better satisfied when everyone knows what to expect or what is expected. You should be careful, also, to include an item in your committee budget for organ music. We should not require the organist to furnish his music any more than we expect this of the choir. Again, however, you will want to require that an up-to-date library of organ music be kept. Incidentally, it is your job to secure a substitute organist or director when your regular staff members are on vacation.

Be sure to show your appreciation to these sometimes forgotten people of the church. Plan a Choir Recognition Sunday or some such event when the congregation will have an opportunity to express their appreciation and their thanks. Most churches have volunteer choirs, but we take these faithful servants for granted after a time. Let it not be so in your church.

4. Other Musical Programs

In addition to special services of music for special occasions, there are some other things you may wish to do. Musical opportunities in your church may include children's choirs, youth choirs, a male chorus, or a quartet. Perhaps you will want to develop such "feeder" choirs that will continually be training voices to move into the chancel choir. Your committee might work with the minister and choir director in featuring special hymns, new hymns, etc., in order to teach them to the congregation. You may want to sponsor services of hymn singing. Promoting the program of music in your church can be a lot of fun.

The Prayer Life of the Congregation

There are many things that you can do, some of them in cooperation with the Home and Family Nurture Subcommittee of the Committee on Strengthening the Church, to encourage and improve the prayer life of your people. Perhaps it would be wise to approach this from the standpoint of the various types of prayer life that you hope to develop.

1. Family Worship

You should see to it that *Day by Day,* the daily devotional booklet of our denomination, is available to members of the congregation. You may wish to provide it free of charge. From time to time (for example, during Christian Family Week) you may wish to sponsor special nights or even courses on the "how" of family worship. Occasional book displays of devotional literature are a spur to families, particularly those with children, who have need for special materials. Some churches provide a special pledge card with the Every Member Canvass, asking their families to pledge to worship together each day in the coming year. There are many ways by which you can stimulate family worship if members of your committee are concerned enough to put their minds to work!

2. Formal Prayer Services

Surely there is a place in the life of the church for services of prayer. Today many churches are attempting to recapture the power of prayer for their congregations through services of prayer. Originally the traditional Wednesday night prayer meeting was just that. How and when you conduct special prayer services will depend on your local situation. A method that is growing in popularity is an early morning prayer service. Although mothers with small children and schoolchildren are excluded by the hour, it does enable the church to reach the working man and woman. Many churches serve a light breakfast afterward for a nominal fee. One church has the people who come take turns serving the meal, and this seems to work out very well. You can think of many more ideas that will fit your local situation. But surely in these days and times there is a tremendous need to lay hold of this source of spiritual power in the life of the church. Such meetings for prayer should include use of the great prayers of the Church, such as those of adoration, confession, thanksgiving, supplication, intercession, and prayer for the sick.

3. Private Worship

An important part of prayer life that should not be ignored is the private worship of the individual. You can encourage such worship through the provision of aids of one sort or another. Books of devotions, Scripture readings, and prayers are helpful to the individual; and by making them available, you will encourage him in his personal growth. Ask your minister to preach on prayer from time to time. Emphasize it in the church paper, in circles of the Women of the Church, and elsewhere. Gentle reminders go a long way.

4. Other Ideas

There are many ways to stimulate interest in prayer and devotional life, and you may want to utilize some of them. For example, you might sponsor cottage prayer meetings, special seasons of prayer (such as the Week of Prayer and Self-Denial for World Missions). During these seasons some churches open their sanctuaries and provide for continuous prayers around the clock. Providing in the bulletin a "prayer of preparation" for worshipers to use when they enter the sanctuary will not only be helpful to them but will also help to create a quiet atmosphere of worship before the service actually begins.

Some General Items

Your committee has plenty to keep it busy over the year! There are other things that will fall to your committee from time to time. For example, you may have (as many churches do) the problem of noisy and irreverent chatter immediately before services. You will want to initiate some program conducive to worship when the people enter the sanctuary. Your committee may be called upon from time to time to provide worship services for special events—such as the laying of a cornerstone, or family night suppers. Other things will be brought to your attention, and you will need to deal with them. Your committee will discover other important tasks in addition to those suggested. Spend some time at each meeting thinking through various phases of your work, and constantly evaluate to be sure each one is receiving adequate attention.

Your committee plays a large part in leading your congregation in worship that is meaningful and real. It is your privilege to direct and guide people into deep, rich spiritual experiences through which they meet and come to know the living Lord. Yours is a solemn responsibility. Enter upon it with reverent humility and continue in it with faithful diligence.

VIII

THE COMMITTEE
ON COMMITMENT

In the past we have thought of commitment primarily in terms of stewardship and finances. And although we have always recognized that the stewardship of time, abilities, and money was a description of total commitment, we have never had an adequate way to tie these things together. However, through the results of our study on Worship and Work, new ways are being devised to serve the local church in developing a program of total commitment. Therefore, this committee will be one of the most vital, meaningful, and useful committees of the Church Session. The primary function of this committee will be to lead the members of the congregation into a deeper commitment that involves all of life: time for Christ's service, talents for His Kingdom, money for His work.

Let us think together for a moment about the meaning of commitment. Who are we thinking about in terms of commitment? Primarily four groups: those who are active in the church, those who belong but are inactive, those who are non-communing members (children of believing parents), and those who are not at present related to the local congregation (this would include non-Christians as well as those who might come by transfer of letter or by reaffirmation of faith). This answers the question of who. The next question is, "What is our concern for these groups of people?" The answer is, "Our concern is to lead them to commitment to Jesus Christ which involves their time, abilities, and money, and which finds expression in all of life."

This means that you will need to develop a program that will enable you to fulfill these responsibilities. First, it will be a program of teaching the meaning of total commitment and helping persons find ways to give expression to their commitment. Therefore, you will want to develop a program that will teach the meaning of commitment of time. This means not only time for work in the program of the church, but learning what it means to say that all of one's time is a gift from God and is to be used for Him. You will need to develop a program to teach the meaning of the use of one's abilities, not only within the covenant community but also in the larger parish of the world in which one lives. Again, you will want to develop a program of teaching the Christian attitude toward money. This means not only developing "the grace of liberality" toward the church, but using all of one's money as a good steward of God's grace. Thus, you are involved in developing a program of total commitment. And as a sort of parenthesis at this point, since such a program of total commitment involves money, there will need to be a close co-operation between your committee and the appropriate committee of the Board of Deacons.

But second, not only will you need to teach total commitment, you will need to teach it to the four different groups of persons mentioned above. This may mean different things for the different groups. Generally, then, your duty as the Committee on Commitment is to lead people into total commitment that involves time, abilities, and money. In addition, other duties involving some phase of commitment will be assigned to you. (In large churches, separate committees may be appointed to take care of these duties.) Another will be the development of the relationship of your church to the presbytery, synod, and General Assembly to ensure that your church will be a good steward of the matters that come to it from these other courts.

With this overview of the total duty of your committee, let us turn now to see how your duties may be spelled out in detail as you attempt to fulfill your ministry.

Deepening the Commitment
of Communing Members

How does one go about helping others to a deeper commitment to Jesus Christ? We will discuss the financial aspects of this commitment later, but how about one's time and abilities? There are a number of ways this can be done, and you will want to use the suggestions of the Resource Guide on Commitment in the annual *Presbyterian Plan Book*. This will include encouraging the minister in a strong pulpit presentation of what it means to be a Christian and a member of the covenant family. It may include creating discussion groups or small Bible study groups to think through the meaning of commitment for one's daily task as well as meeting responsibility within the church itself. Perhaps in conjunction with the annual Every Member Canvass you will want to canvass the congregation to make a stewardship analysis of their talents. You might use a "talent inventory" (such as the John Knox Record Card) which would give them opportunity to list the things the members can do or are interested in being trained to do. Another idea would be to list the various jobs and opportunities for service available in your congregation and actively go out to challenge people to accept those responsibilities. There are many methods you can use to lead persons to deeper commitment, and each year the Resource Guide on Commitment will carry new and additional suggestions. The important thing is to be aware of the nature of your duty and to develop a program to fulfill it.

Leading Non-Communing Members
to Commitment

Within your church there are those who have been baptized as infants but have not yet made their personal commitment to Jesus Christ as Lord and Saviour. It is your job to help them to that commitment. How can you do this? One possibility is to have a communicants' class for youth (and children, depending on the ages for which your Session has determined it will offer such a class). There is a great deal of material available to help you in planning a meaningful class.

Another possibility is to follow a procedure for which special material has been created in the Covenant Life Curriculum. This plan recognizes the fact that the young person, his parents, the pastor, and the Session all have distinctive roles to play as the young person faces the matter of Christian decision. Three booklets, having a common title, have been prepared to provide guidance in this preparation of youth for communicant membership. They are the following:

> Youth Entering into Covenant: For Youth, by J. Will Ormond
> Youth Entering into Covenant: For Pastor and Session, by J. Will Ormond
> Youth Entering into Covenant: For Parents, by William A. Benfield, Jr.[1]

Helping New Members
to a Beginning Commitment

There will be several types of new members coming into your fellowship. These will include persons making a profession of faith for the first time, those coming by transfer from other churches (and other denominations), and those who are coming by reaffirmation or by restoration to the active roll. As these people enter your covenant family, one of the things you will want to do for all of them is to offer a class on the meaning of church membership and the meaning of commitment. Such a class should include also a study of doctrine, government, and a brief history of the Presbyterian Church. We do a disservice to the church and to those we are seeking to unite with it if we fail to make clear to them what we believe and what we will expect of them as members of our church. Resource materials include the *Communicants' Class Kit*[2] and *Into Covenant Life*.[3]

---

1. Listed on the Covenant Life Curriculum order blank, these are to be secured from the Department of Curriculum Distribution, Box 1176, Richmond, Virginia 23209.

2. *Communicants' Class Kit.* This basic resource includes the book *Toward Responsible Discipleship*, by William B. Ward; *Leader's Resources*

Caring for New Members

As new members come into your church, they usually will know very few other members. They will not be familiar with the work and worship of your church. Only as they become a real part of your fellowship will they make good church members. This is part of your job. Assimilating a person or a family into the church is not an easy job. It takes work. Again, it will demand some record-keeping on your part in order that you may know what is happening in the life of a particular person. Appendix E is a form used by one church to keep up with new members over a six-month period. It has some features you may wish to incorporate into your program, although this particular form might not meet your need.

1. Letter from the Pastor

A warm, friendly letter from the pastor, expressing some of his hopes for the new members as they take their place in the church, gets a new member started off on the right foot.

2. New-Member Packet

You will want to develop a packet of materials for new members. It should include a list of the church's monthly activities, a membership roll, a certificate of membership, a pledge card and offering envelopes, an interest-finder and family information sheet to be returned to the church office for your information in setting up a permanent record, and other literature you consider helpful. Some suggestions would be tithing material, family worship material (with a copy of *Day by Day* and the *Presbyterian Survey*), local church history, and so forth.

3. Orientation Session

A special orientation session should be held for the new mem-

---

for *Adult Communicants' Classes,* by Mac and Anne Turnage; a color filmstrip showing the history of the Church; and two twelve-inch records to be used with the filmstrip. Available from Presbyterian Book Stores.

3. *Into Covenant Life,* by William B. Kennedy. Introduction course for adults. Available from Presbyterian Book Stores.

bers. Perhaps you will want to have a dinner for them (along with their neighborhood family—see next paragraph), at which you will interpret your church and its program to them. Such a meeting should provide some opportunity for questions as well. Some excellent filmstrips on the meaning of church membership are available.[4] Several experiments may be necessary in order to work out the program that best suits your situation. Such a program gives new members an opportunity to meet each other and get acquainted with the church staff, as well as to learn about their new church home.

4. Neighborhood Families

How about assigning a new family to an active church family who live in the same neighborhood? Make them responsible for visiting with the new family and introducing them into various phases of the church program, bringing them to church school and other gatherings for a certain period. You may want to assign this duty to an Elder and his family. In addition, you will want your pastor to visit, as well as the Director of Christian Education if you have one. Many new members rightly complain that they are visited regularly until they join the church and then are dropped "like a hot potato"!

5. Notifying Other Groups

Other organizations within the church should be told about the new family. For example, every church school class in which a member of the new family belongs should be notified. And your committee should follow up to see that each member of the family has been contacted by a church school class. Men of the Church, Women of the Church, youth groups, the choir, Scouts, and other organizations should be notified. Your objective is to get every member of the family involved in meaningful phases of the life and work of the church. If their interest sheet data in-

---

4. Filmstrips for communicant classes include "The Beginnings of Christianity"; "The Beginnings of Presbyterianism"; and "The Beginnings of the Presbyterian Church, U. S." These are available from the Presbyterian Book Stores.

dicate special talents, committees that can use a particular talent should be notified.

6. A Continuing Check

Do not take it for granted that all these things happen; check to make sure. If you keep a continuing record on a new family for a few months, you will be up to date on what is happening to them and can determine whether they need additional attention or whether they have found a place in the church. For example, find out if the family is pledging and if not, why not. Are they attending church school? Sunday services? Other organizations? On the basis of such questions as these, you will decide whether they need additional help in finding a place for themselves in your church family.

This sounds like a great deal of work. It is! However, to help a person become a useful member of the kingdom of God is something that takes planning and work. Each year our denomination takes in many new members. Unfortunately, it loses almost as many. As has been truly said, the greatest field of evangelism is the church. We can stop this exodus out the back door of the church by being concerned for our old members and by keeping up with what is happening to their spiritual life. We can stop it as we train our new members to be good churchmen from the very beginning. This is a major part of your responsibility.

Enlistment of Leaders

Because your committee has the duty to develop the commitment of members, it is only logical that you would serve the entire congregation as a personnel committee. As we have mentioned above, you will want to challenge persons in your fellowship (both "old" members and new) to commitment that involves time and talents in the service of the church. We have already suggested that you use the John Knox Record Card as an inventory of talents for both new and old members. From this you have a resource to enable you to find persons who are qualified and willing to do particular jobs. Probably you will want to prepare a master list of persons who are working in the church so that you can work especially to use those who are not presently serving. Also, such a master list will help you avoid overworking those who are serving. Most churches have a "hard core" group whose members are always willing to serve. We tend to use them too much and never challenge those who are not giving of time and talents. It is your job, then, not only to make use of available persons who are qualified and willing to serve, but also to develop new leadership and, in co-operation with the Committee on Strengthening the Church, to give them proper training. A helpful manual, *The Enlistment of Leaders for the Work of the Church,* is available from the Department of Curriculum Distribution, Board of Christian Education.

Your sights need to be higher than just the local congregation, however. You should be alert to those who can be challenged to full-time Christian service as ministers, missionaries, Directors of Christian Education, or in other church-related occupations. There are a large number of resources available to you on this which you can get from the Department of Enlistment, Board of Christian Education.

Expressing Commitment in Vocation

We have talked about commitment of time and abilities and have said that this means more than working in the church, for it involves one's whole life. One of the great doctrines of the Reformation has to do with vocation. By this we understand that wherever a person is and whatever job he is doing, it is there that God calls that person to live before Him and to serve Him. Therefore, it is your duty to help persons understand that their place of daily work is the place where they are living before God and are influencing society by their lives.

And what about those young boys and girls who are thinking about their life's work? Here, too, it is your job to help them understand the meaning of vocation and to give them guidance and counsel as they seek to find God's will in choosing the occupation in which they can best serve. In helping young people, our denomination offers you an outstanding program. It is called the Presbyterian Guidance Program and offers practical means of guiding youth in the vital decision on their choice of a career. If you do not already know about this excellent program, you will want to send for the introductory pamphlet "Vocational Guidance for Christian Youth" (available free from the Department of Christian Vocation, Board of Christian Education) and the *Presbyterian Guidance Program Handbook* (order from the Presbyterian Book Store nearest you).

The Commitment of Money

Money is an inevitable part of one's total commitment. Therefore, even as you have a year-round program of commitment involving time and abilities, there should also be a year-round program of commitment that involves money. Suggestions for such a continuing program are provided in "Stewardship Education and Enlistment in the Local Church" (available from the General Council, Presbyterian Church, U. S., 341 Ponce de Leon Avenue, N.E., Atlanta, Georgia 30308). This is an excellent development of a suggested program and should be indispensable to you.

Actually, the responsibility for the finances of the church rests upon the Board of Deacons only in limited degree. The Book of Church Order states in Section 12-3 that the Board must have the Session's approval of the regular budget as well as approval in other important financial matters. In addition, the Session has a joint responsibility with the Board of Deacons for the planning of financial objectives. The Session may also aid the Board by appointing "godly women" to assist in the collection and distribution of gifts (§ 12-7). This authority is in addition to the fact that women may now be elected to serve as Deacons. Again, as has been pointed out elsewhere in this book, since money is basic to program, and since the program is the responsibility of the Session, the Session must be responsible for policy decisions involving the finances of the church. Therefore, since one's commitment of his finances is a part of his total commitment, and since your committee is responsible for the program of total commitment, it is your duty to work with the Deacons in developing a year-round program of stewardship that fits into your committee's over-all program of commitment.

Your committee should co-operate with the Board of Deacons in formulating the method of challenging the people of your congregation to render a *full* stewardship to the Lord. This will include co-operating in the Every Member Canvass program, as well as in special seasons of stewardship emphasis such as the Christmas Joy Gift and the Easter offering for Overseas Relief. In conjunction with the Budget Committee of the Board, you will need to be conscious of the giving habits of your congregation and of the individual families within it, working to lead them to the tithe as a means of growth in commitment. (See the report on the tithe, Minutes of the General Assembly, 1961, pages 126-132.) Also, you will want to know the per capita giving of your congregation, particularly as it relates to benevolence contributions. As a matter of policy, special benevolence askings should be channeled through your committee. Strive to have your church share in the benevolences of the denomination at every level to the best of its ability.

Matters of Policy

Many matters will come to your attention that will require the establishment of a policy. For example, a question may arise concerning the use of church equipment off the premises, or its use by non-church groups. While you probably will leave individual cases with the Property Committee of the Board of Deacons, the policy decision belongs to the Session alone (§ 15-6 (10)). In some churches even today, in spite of our efforts to teach the proper methods of church support, there is still the problem of groups within the church desiring to use various means to raise money which are outside our tradition. As far back as 1888 (Minutes of the General Assembly, page 402), our Church spoke out against such schemes to secure money for church purposes and expressed the view that "giving should be an act of worship, and thus a means of grace." Your committee will be responsible for formulating policies on such matters for recommendation to the Session. Again, you may wish to establish a policy concerning benevolence payments. For example, you might recommend that the first 25 percent of each week's offerings will be paid to benevolences. There are many and varied areas in which policy decisions will have to be made. Your committee will be responsible for being conscious of those areas and will make needed recommendations to the Session. Quite often groups or individuals go to the minister with special requests. It is not fair to ask him to make a decision which belongs to the Session; and he should be able to refer such requests to your committee with confidence, knowing that they will be properly handled.

Oversight of Other Organizations

Since the Session is responsible for the oversight of the total program of the church, it will fall to the Committee on Commitment to be responsible for relating the work of other organizations to the total life of the church. Therefore, you will want to co-operate with the Women of the Church, the Men of the Church, the Scouts, and other groups who meet under the auspices of the church. In addition, your Session may assign to you the oversight of the work of other church-related groups. Since it is vitally important that such groups fulfill the purpose for which they were created, you will want to be diligent in your oversight of these programs and relate them to your total program in a meaningful way.

Memorials

Most churches today have some sort of Memorial Fund for the reception of gifts. This duty will fall under your committee. Be certain that gifts are acknowledged to the donor. Probably you will want to have some formal card to notify the family that a gift has been made in honor of their loved one, giving the name of the donor. As you accumulate these funds, your committee will want to select some object that will be suitable and in keeping with the spirit of those who gave and that will appropriately memorialize those honored. Also, it will be helpful if there is a current list of suitable memorial objects that can be given by those who desire.

Summary

The area of responsibility assigned to you by the Session is an important one. All the possibilities have by no means been exhausted. Spend some time with your committee in thinking through all the areas of commitment that belong to you. The more your committee and your church give of yourselves, the more you will be the Church.

IX

THE COMMITTEE
ON WITNESS

The Committee on Witness is the arm of the Church reaching out into the world. Its work is the expression in the local congregation of the mission of the Church, to win the world for Christ. Through the outreach of evangelism, there is a transfusing of new life into the continuing Church, keeping it virile and strong through the centuries. The importance of the work of your committee cannot be overstressed. This is not the place to discuss the motive for evangelism, but surely your committee could spend some fruitful hours together discussing this subject. The evangelistic effort of the Church has always stumbled when those engaged in it have not been fully committed or have not fully understood what they were doing. Unless your committee has a firm grasp of why you are seeking to win others to Christ, it can never do an adequate job. May we suggest that your committee read several good books on the subject.[1]

The task of your committee is relatively simple compared to that of other committees of the Session, primarily because your area of responsibility is more clearly defined. This does not mean that it is easier or that it will take less planning and work. It does mean that you can concentrate the efforts of your committee more fully on what you will be doing. What are your general duties? First of all you are to seek the fruits of the preached Word and inform the pastor of cases of awakening. This means that you will have the task of being the evangelistic

---

1. Two books that will help you are *Effective Evangelism* by George E. Sweazey and *The Witnessing Community* by Suzanne de Dietrich, obtainable from your Presbyterian Book Store.

arm of your congregation. In addition you will have the task of relating your church to the program of church extension both locally and across the denomination. And the other large task that falls under your committee duty is to relate your church to the larger evangelism program of our denomination in world missions. Let us look at possible ways of accomplishing these and other phases of your noble task.[2]

The Task of Evangelism

Not only must we seek out those whose hearts are being awakened under the preaching ministry of the Church, but we must also seek out those who are not relating themselves to Jesus Christ and His Church. How shall we go about the task of finding these people? There are many ways to do this. Your committee should sit down and think through the various ways of contacting for Christ those people who are new in your community or who are unrelated to any church. Let us look briefly at some of the major methods of obtaining names.

1. Visitor Registration

A guest book at the main entrance to the church, with a warm, friendly person to greet visitors and register them, is always good. A book for such use is available at your Presbyterian Book Store. The greeter should be neat and attractive and should know how to welcome strangers. In addition, such a person should know the congregation well enough to be able to recognize a visitor. Another method, used by many churches, is to have a registration form in the pew and have visitors (or even all the worshipers) register at some point in the service, giving name and address and church affiliation. We recommend a registration of everyone present, as the registration of church members can be used by other committees in the pastoral oversight of the congregation.

---

2. The Division of Evangelism of the Board of Church Extension, 341-B Ponce de Leon Avenue, N. E., Atlanta, Georgia 30308, will provide upon request the materials available.

2. Surveys

One method for securing the names of those unchurched or new to a community is a house-to-house survey of specific areas. Plans for setting up such a survey are available from the Division of Evangelism. Although this method may be helpful in some areas, particularly new ones, it has been used so often by all denominations that its value in established areas is now somewhat lessened. The amount of organization and work involved in carrying on such a program is tremendous; and probably your efforts could be spent in more meaningful and fruitful channels.

3. Using Your Own Members

Your own members are a valuable source for the names of new and unchurched families. If this method is emphasized through the church paper, weekly bulletin, and other means, your congregation can be educated to be on the lookout for new families and unchurched families in their neighborhood. A printed card for reporting such families, placed in the pew rack, will pay dividends.

4. The Church School

Your church school attendance records will be a valuable source of information. There will be children—and even adults —in your church school who are not affiliated with your church. Make a list of these and visit them systematically with a view to winning them to Christ and His Church.

5. Professional Services

For those in large cities, there are professional services that will provide the names of new residents for a nominal fee. This service can be of tremendous use, particularly when the denomination of the new resident is listed. Often in the smaller communities the utilities companies, Chambers of Commerce, or Merchants Association will make available the names and addresses of new residents.

Calling on Prospects

With a supply of names, with a need to be met, and with a job to do, how will you go about it? That is the next question that confronts your committee. Let us look at the major problems involved in setting up a program of visitation evangelism.

1. Selecting Your Method

The first thing you will need to decide on is your method of making calls. There are numerous means at your disposal. Discuss them and then decide on the ones that best fit your situation. One method is through an Andrew Club. This is an organization of men (or men and women) who meet together at stated times (weekly or monthly, perhaps) to receive assignments and make calls. Another good method is to ask a family to serve as an evangelism unit, giving them another family to win for Christ and His Church. In addition, you might have an all women's group who would do visiting, say, during the morning hours when the wife is at home and relatively free to sit and talk about her family and the Church. Some churches have a monthly meeting to which those interested in calling come for assignments. Think through the various ways visiting can be done and select the method or methods that suit your situation best.

2. Selecting the Visitors

Having determined the "how," you must now determine the "who." Decide first on what you desire in a visitor. There are some well-intentioned persons who will volunteer for calling but who are simply not capable of doing it effectively. You will want to be careful in establishing qualifications and in selecting persons to fit them. After you have made a list of persons who fit your qualifications, you should contact them personally. Explain the job you are asking them to undertake. Be sure they fully understand the nature of the task and what it is you are asking them to do. You will have better visitors that way.

3. Training Visitors

After you have determined your method and selected your

visitors, you should offer some training to the callers. Much material is available to you through the Division of Evangelism. Your pastor will be of special help in this training process. Your visitation teams should have adequate training, not only in the techniques of visiting but also in the motives for evangelism. Spend some time in these training sessions, for it will prove beneficial in the long run.

4. Using Materials in Visiting

You may find it invaluable to make up a packet of materials for use by teams in visiting the unchurched. Such materials are a means of interpreting your church to prospective members. You may want to create a piece of literature on your own local church to use in this way. Many leaflets are available to help you along this line, but you will want to use them wisely and well. Be careful not to deluge people with materials. Literature is no substitute for well-trained visitors who are genuinely concerned.

Initial Contacts

Before your visitation team ever calls on a family, there may be some initial contacts that you will want to make with them. For example, if you use some form of newcomer service or other method of acquiring the names of new residents, a letter from your church will be helpful. Such a letter might enclose a map showing the location of your church and giving a list of the church's activities. Again, if the family has already visited your church, a warm, friendly letter from the minister will go a long way toward making them feel that they were welcome and preparing them for the visit of a team. If members of the family have visited church school classes, a card or telephone call from the teachers (especially to the children) is helpful in letting them know you are interested in them. There are many ways of making an initial contact that will prepare the way for your visitation teams. Think through all of them and decide on the ones you will use.

A Continuing Concern

One visit will rarely win people for Christ and the Church. It usually takes a continued effort on your part. What are some of the things your committee can do to show a continued interest in a family? Your committee will want to work this out for themselves, but let us look briefly at some of the major ways.

1. Continued Visiting

A family should be called on a second time even if they have not attended church since the first call. Also, you should keep a continuing record on each family and how they respond to your visits. We suggest a simple card record file, giving the names and address of the family and how you secured their name. On that card should be listed the date of the call, the names of the callers, and a brief summary of the visit. Vital information such as church background, church affiliation, and approximate ages should be placed on this card. Avoid calling too frequently on one family, but be diligent to see that they are called on more than once.

2. Other Contacts

There are other things your committee can do to show your interest and to stimulate interest as well. For example, you might want to put your prospective members on the mailing list for your church paper or other mailings of general interest. You should be sure that the church school maintains a continuing interest in the family. Use other organizations in the church in your efforts. For example, give names to the Men and Women of the Church and have them invite prospects to meetings. Use your young people in "youth-to-youth" evangelism. There are numerous ways to maintain a continuing contact and concern.

Making Your Church Friendly

One of the most important things in evangelism is the atmosphere of your church. If it is warm and friendly, so that strangers feel welcome and at home, the hardest part of your work is done. Therefore, your committee will want to help create and stimulate this atmosphere. Encourage your people to speak to strangers. Some churches use a form of name tag or ribbon to identify visitors so members can recognize them easily. A greeter at the door is a help. Some congregations have a coffee period before or after church at which visitors are welcomed and made to feel at home. But whatever you do, seek to make yours a friendly church. Encourage church school classes to recognize visitors and welcome them. Train your people to watch for strangers and to greet all visitors. Being a friendly church doesn't just happen; you have to work at it!

Other Helps to Evangelism

We have by no means exhausted the avenues available to your committee. For example, in co-operation with the Committee on Commitment you might want to offer a class on membership for interested persons. A course on what Presbyterians believe is helpful in leading persons to make a definite decision for Christ. Such a course could include a brief history of the Presbyterian Church, the beliefs of the Church, understanding the sacraments of the Church, the government and organization of the Church (both locally and nationally), principles of stewardship in the Presbyterian Church (see particularly the report on the tithe in the Minutes of the General Assembly, 1961, pages 126-132), and opportunities for service in the church.

From time to time you may need to remind yourselves, as well as those you lead, that we witness to Christ most effectively through our attitudes and actions in everyday life. In all phases of your task, use your imagination and be willing to work. With these two ingredients, your church can be led in an effective program of evangelism. It will take dedication, commitment, and much prayer; but the goal is more than worth the effort.

The Task of Church Extension

Part of your job will be to help the congregation assume its responsibility for the witness of the Church at home. This may well include supplying destitute places with the regular ministry of the Word. In most Presbyteries, the Commission on the Minister and His Work assumes the responsibility for working with churches without pastors, to help them fill their pulpits. However, in consultation with the Committee on Worship you can aid the Commission by providing the names of Elders from your church who are capable of conducting worship services for such churches. In some areas it may be that a larger church can serve smaller churches and new missions by providing someone to preach and conduct services of divine worship. Investigate the situation in your community and determine whether there is such a need that can be met by your church. In co-operation with the Committee on Worship, arrange to use qualified men in your own church when possible, such as at evening services, on Laymen's Sunday, and when there are other opportunities to develop them in preaching so that they will be qualified to serve when the need and opportunity arise.

Other activities of your committee in the field of church extension will include observance of the Church Extension Season, developing interest in new churches, and many other areas of concern. You will find helpful suggestions and ideas, along with suggested resource materials, in your Resource Guide on Witness. This guide is published as a part of the *Presbyterian Plan Book* each year. You will want to consult it for further program ideas.

The Task of World Missions

Another area of responsibility assigned to your committee is that of making your congregation aware of the world mission task of our denomination and helping the members to become aware of their role in that mission. This will include such things as sponsoring a school of missions, observing the Week of Prayer and Self-Denial for World Missions, confronting youth and adults with specialized training with the opportunity for enlisting personally in the missionary service overseas, promoting and encouraging attendance at such events as the World Missions Conference at Montreat, and caravans to the Mexican missions. For additional ideas and suggestions in making your people aware of their world missions, consult the Resource Guide on Witness.[3]

A Summary of Your Task

Your primary job is that of evangelism within your own local situation. Yet, you should not become so involved in your own program that you fail to see in good perspective your church's share in the task of witnessing at home and around the world. It is true that your immediate concern is within your own situation as you attempt to reach others for Christ. But if you fail to help your people become involved in the larger task of evangelism, you will have done them a disservice in the long run. Therefore, to have an adequate program of witness involves much more than evangelism in your own community. Your committee will have done an effective job of witnessing not only when it has brought others to a faith in and commitment to Jesus Christ, but also when it has developed in your congregation a sense of responsibility for and participation in the wider witness of the Church both at home and abroad.

---

3. The Educational Department of the Board of World Missions, P. O. Box 330, Nashville, Tennessee 37202, will provide specific suggestions and materials upon request.

X

THE COMMITTEE ON SERVICE

The Session is charged with the spiritual oversight of the local congregation. This is one of the most neglected areas within most churches. It is either left entirely to the minister or is simply ignored by many Sessions; yet it is a critical area in the life of the church. Most Church Sessions have some program of education and do at least some evangelistic work. But the Session has an equally heavy responsibility in the spiritual care of those who are already a part of the church family. This committee is charged with watching diligently over the congregation, visiting the sick, comforting the bereaved, and keeping the pastor aware of the "afflicted" of the community—those with special needs. The committee should feel a concern for the conduct of those under its care and devise suitable measures for advancing the spiritual interests of the congregation. In addition, the committee will be charged not only with care of its own members, but with care for others as well. Such care will include Christian action in needed areas as well as aid and care for those with special needs.

This area is tremendously important in the life of the church, and it deserves the care and concern of a dedicated committee. As the members of your group sit down to think through what is required of them, they will discover the magnitude of their responsibility. Your problem will be to discover adequate ways of meeting that responsibility. You might plan to emphasize a particular need each year. If inactive members are your present problem, work hardest at that. If you are a new church in a new area, you will want to concentrate on new member assimilation.

As we begin to specify some of the duties before you, remember that this brief chapter cannot begin to exhaust the possibilities that are open to you. Let this be a suggestive guide to what you can and will do.

Spiritual Care of Members

As you watch over the congregation committed to your care, there are numerous things you will want to do to ensure their spiritual health and growth. However, in order to have some idea of the spiritual vitality of a particular person or family, you will need to know what is happening to them.

1. *Attendance and Participation*

It will be helpful to your committee to keep a continuing record of the attendance and participation of every family in your congregation. In order to do this, you will need some method of recording such activity. In co-operation with the Committee on Witness, you may initiate some form of registration for all members who attend the worship services of the church. A careful record of this attendance should be kept, for in many cases it will serve as a basis for action by your committee. For example, as you record a particular family's attendance, you may discover that they have missed church four Sundays in a row. This is a warning signal to you. Evidently there is sickness in the family, or interest is waning, or something has gone wrong in the life of this family. In any case, you will want to act.

As you work with your people, it will be well also to have a permanent, continuing record of the religious life of each family. Although it will demand a great deal of work and effort, you must remember that your concern is people. Unless you know what is happening to them, you cannot minister to them. Such a record could include attendance at church and church school, participation in church activities, and visits made by pastor or Session. Some such form will be of great value to your committee members as they begin their work and will help them to become well acquainted with every member.

2. Caring for Special Needs

As you begin to go over the families of your congregation, you will discover that some of them have special needs. For example, you may discover a husband whose wife is not a member of any church. In such cases as these, when only part of a family belongs to the church, the Committee on Witness should be notified. Some other special needs would include the sick (and the bereaved). Those who are ill should have some special attention and care, not only from the pastor but from the Session as well. Another group that your committee will want to consider is the shut-ins. These people deserve and need special care. They need to be visited regularly; and perhaps you will want to have some form of home church school developed for them in co-operation with your Committee on Strengthening the Church. Special projects that are within their capabilities and are genuinely meaningful should be planned for them. Another group that needs special attention is our senior citizens. Many of them are able to be relatively active, but often they are lonely. Some special activities should be planned for this group. They are a valuable source of manpower for work within the church, including some of the mailing and other office routines, and should be used as much as possible. Your committee should think through what it can do for them and what they can do for the church.

3. Inactive Members

The records you keep on church families are not an end in themselves. As information, records are useless unless they can be an aid in ministering to the needs of people. In spite of your best efforts, some of your families, for one reason or another, will become inactive. These persons need special attention, and your committee in co-operation with the Committee on Commitment should give it to them. Visit them to find out what the problem is, and then attempt to deal with that problem. Your minister will be of great assistance here. Also, you will want to see that they are visited regularly in an effort to reclaim them for Christ. There is not much point in the Committee on Witness working to get members in the front door if others are going out the back door just as fast! Your committee should deal realistically with this problem and establish a workable program that will close the back door. You can do this by setting up visitation teams, by asking one family to take on an inactive family as a special project, or by using some other method.

This means that of your regular church members, you have at least three classes of members who need special attention in terms of visitation. Perhaps you will want to start a "Good Shepherd" visitation group of several couples who will willingly work with those persons—the shut-ins, the sick, and the inactive. In addition, such a group could visit new members as well.

Service to Those in Need

One of your duties will be to help your congregation become concerned about human need and suffering and lead them in taking appropriate action to meet or relieve that need. For example, from available surveys, reports, and other sources that are available from the public library or county health and welfare department or other agency, you can discover needs in your community that you may not dream exist, and you will want to lead your congregation in taking some appropriate action. You might want to talk to leaders in various areas of community life and discover from them some of the problems in your community that you might take part in solving. Your job might be simply to make your congregation aware of the needs and encourage individual participation in community agencies to solve these problems, or you might want to organize some particular activity through which your own congregation can meet the need you have discovered. You will want to consult the Resource Guide on Service to be found in the *Presbyterian Plan Book*. There you will find many suggestions to guide you as you plan a program of Christian action that reaches out to your own particular community and across the land and the world.

Action to Remove Causes of Need

A major responsibility of the committee will be in leading the congregation to an understanding of the causes of human need and suffering and in taking action to eliminate these causes. In every generation there are social evils which bring inexpressible hurt to persons by offending both body and spirit. Too often the Church has been content to treat the symptoms of community evil without diagnosing and attacking the causes. Thus, for example, a detention home will be built for delinquent youth without any move to prevent delinquency by giving youth an environment in which to grow into clean manhood and womanhood. Or, again, an effort will be made to give training to an unemployed person, often a member of a minority racial group, without working for the correction of an unjust social custom or structure which deprived him of an adequate education in the first place. Obviously, as Christians you will be concerned with the causes as well as the effects of social evils. Areas of concern which demand the attention and action of your committee will include economic life, politics, alcohol and narcotics, crime and delinquency, gambling, and international affairs. Again, your Resource Guide on Service will be of invaluable aid to you as you think through specific areas that need the action of concerned Christians. Ask the Holy Spirit to guide you in leading your congregation to become aware of the problems of our time and to seek ways of meeting them.

XI

THE COMMITTEE ON STRENGTHENING THE CHURCH

If the Committee on Strengthening the Church is not the most important committee in the local church, at least there is no committee *more* important! In addition to the suggestions that are to be found in the Resource Guide on Strengthening the Church there is much helpful information and material available for the work of this committee from our Board of Christian Education. You can secure what you need by writing that Board at Box 1176, Richmond, Virginia 23209. In this chapter we shall give a sort of "overview" of the total area of responsibility of this committee to give you the broad perspective of your task in strengthening the church. The methods and techniques that you will use in fulfilling these various duties will be left largely up to you.

The broad scope of responsibility for this committee will be the nurture of the members of the congregation, young and old, and training them for responsible life and service in the church and in the world. Your committee will assist the Session in developing and supervising the formal educational program of the church as well as the ministry of home and family nurture. It will also have the general responsibility for providing for leadership training, including the training of church officers as required by the Book of Church Order.

Because of this committee's particular responsibilities it should become thoroughly familiar with the Covenant Life Curriculum, the authorized curriculum of the Presbyterian Church in the United States, which provides guidance and materials both for the church school and for home and family nurture. We would caution you against using materials other than those produced by our own denomination and remind you that curriculum materials must be approved by the Session of your local church. Unless you are theologically trained, you run the serious risk of exposing your church members to material which is doctrinally unsound and educationally inferior. Any members of the committee who have not already done so should study *Education for Covenant Living*,[1] a popular introduction to the Covenant Life Curriculum, and *Into Covenant Life* (the pupil's edition),[2] the introductory study for adults, as a means of becoming acquainted with the curriculum recommended for our church. There are also various other materials available to provide specific help for the committee in understanding and planning its work in the two areas of systematic study and home and family nurture.[3] The Synod's Director of Christian Education may be consulted for needed assistance and for the latest information about useful resources.

Home and Family Nurture

In spite of the fact that it has been customary to speak of the home as a strategic agency in Christian nurture, the fact is that the notion has widely prevailed that the task of Christian education is chiefly the responsibility of the church school. Parents have acted on the assumption that they could turn over to the church the responsibility for training their children in spiritual matters. Moreover, the significant place that the home actually occupies in the Christian nurture of persons of all ages, adults as well as children, has to a large extent been overlooked. And, further, the responsibility of the Christian family to function as a part of the church in bearing a Christian witness and engaging

---

1. *Education for Covenant Living* (Richmond: Board of Christian Education, Presbyterian Church in the United States, 1962).
2. William Bean Kennedy, *Into Covenant Life,* Volumes I and II (Richmond: The CLC Press, 1963).
3. We suggest that you begin with the manual, *The School of the Church,* by Jack B. McMichael (Richmond: The CLC Press, 1963), and with the manual, *Home and Family Nurture,* by Richard F. Perkins (Richmond: The CLC Press, 1963).

in Christian service in the world has been neglected. With the development of the home and family nurture aspect of the Covenant Life Curriculum, a ministry to homes that will help to equip them for their distinctive responsibility has become possible.

The following quotation from the Home and Family Nurture manual will serve to indicate the directions in which this aspect of the Covenant Life Curriculum proposes to move:

> The specific nature and purpose of the curriculum for Home and Family Nurture can be seen in light of what it hopes to accomplish.
>
> 1. *The curriculum is designed to help families develop a strong core of spiritual strength.* . . .
>
> 2. *The curriculum is designed to help families face and deal with the specific problems which they share as Christians in contemporary society.* . . .
>
> 3. *The curriculum is designed to help families understand, accept, and fufill their responsibilities for homes and families beyond their own.* . . .[4]

The responsibility for the home and family ministry may be carried by the committee as a whole, or it may seem wise because of its great importance to assign the responsibility to a subcommittee. In many churches it may be desirable to have a special committee appointed for this work. Before any permanent assignment of responsibility is made, however, the Session is advised to appoint a temporary committee to work with the pastor in leading the congregation through the first two stages of a recommended strategy for introducing the Home and Family Nurture aspect of the curriculum. Suggestions for a series of stages (including the first two already referred to) in the procedure for leading a church into this aspect of the curriculum will be found in the Home and Family Nurture manual when revised. The first several stages of the strategy are also described in a paper entitled, "Outline of Strategy for Introducing the Home and Family Nurture Aspect of the Covenant Life Curriculum," available from the Synod's Regional Direc-

---

4. Richard F. Perkins, *Home and Family Nurture* (Richmond: The CLC Press, 1963), pages 11-12.

tor of Christian Education, or from the Department of Christian Family Education of the Board of Christian Education.

In planning for home and family nurture the Session should follow the recommended steps in sequence and carry out the suggestions offered at each stage.

The School of the Church

A second major responsibility of your committee is the program of education carried on through the church's school. The Covenant Life Curriculum, with its call for the kind of serious study that too often has been missing heretofore and with its concern that all adults be involved in study in order to be informed and responsible church members, has magnified the place of the school in the life of the church. It has suggested that a new term might well be used to reflect this new emphasis, the term "school of the church."

It is the responsibility of your committee to enable the Session to give to this phase of the educational program the kind of direction its importance demands. Your committee will need to consult the manual, *The School of the Church,* for details relating to operation of the school, but an indication may be given here of some of the matters with which your committee will need to be concerned.

1. The Organization of the School of the Church

In place of the departmental organization that has been common heretofore, it is now recommended that there be four age-group divisions: the preschool division for children from birth to six years of age; the elementary division for children in grades 1 through 6; the youth division for young people in grades 7 through 12; and the adult division, which would include college students with other adults. It is not recommended that a school should have more than these four basic units. Where circumstances seem to call for it, certain divisions may be combined, so that it would be possible for a school to have a children's division, a youth division, and an adult division. A very small school might have a children's division and a combined youth-adult division.

The administrative group for the school is the Church School Council. Its function is that of co-ordinating and giving unity to the work of the divisions of the school and relating the school as a whole to your committee. The Council includes the superintendent as chairman, all associate and assistant superintendents, the division chairmen, and the pastor. The Minister of Education or Director of Christian Education should also have membership on the Council.

Each division of the school should have its own division council to develop and co-ordinate the educational program of the groups in the division and relate its work to that of the whole school through the School Council.

2. Materials and Activities

The Book of Church Order (§ 218-5) includes this statement with reference to the formal educational program of the church: "All materials and activities shall be approved by the Session, and should be in harmony with the educational program approved by the General Assembly." Materials used in the school must be approved by the Session. No teacher or officer is free to use whatever curriculum materials he may personally prefer. The choice of such literature must be made by the Session.

The authorized curriculum for the Presbyterian Church in the United States is the Covenant Life Curriculum. For the time being there are also available for adults, and for certain other age-groups, materials published by our Church in the Uniform Lesson Series. The Covenant Life Curriculum is recommended as much more adequate than the Uniform Series, but in any case the decision on what materials to use is one to be made by the Session. Obviously, the decision should be made on the basis of a careful study.

3. Space and Equipment in the School

The Book of Church Order specifically states that the Session has the responsibility for seeing that adequate buildings and other physical equipment are provided for the school (see § 218-5). Ordinarily the Church School Council will make the room assignments to the various groups in the school, and should make budget requests to cover the cost of the supplies and equipment necessary for successful teaching. Your committee should give every encouragement to efforts to secure proper housing and equipment for the school. In addition to the direct values to be gained from attractive rooms and good equipment, there are indirect values for teaching which result. The church that provides well for the material needs of its school impresses students with the fact that it considers Christian education important. And such an investment encourages leaders themselves to make a solid investment of time and energy.

4. The School Staff

It is the Session's duty to "confirm the choice and appointment of all persons who are to serve in the educational program" (§ 218-5). A recommended procedure for the nomination and election of members of the school staff will be found in the manual, *The Enlistment of Leaders for the Work of the Church.* Your committee should also consult *The School of the Church,* a manual previously referred to. There are two sections of the manual that should be noted in connection with the selection of the school staff. One of the sections begins on page 20 and outlines steps in securing leadership, starting with the preparation of job descriptions for the positions on the church school staff. The other section is on page 40 and indicates how the superintendent is to function in securing suggestions of persons for positions and in making nominations. For your information and guidance a sample job analysis for a church school superintendent (including one for a church school secretary) is given in Appendix C. You should remember that such an analysis is never definitive, since it is geared to a particular church to meet special and unique needs. While you may want to use this one as a guide, your job analysis should reflect your own local situation and be geared to meet *your* unique needs.

The Program for Children and Youth

While the school provides a regularly scheduled program of systematic study for children and youth, there are special features of the program for children and youth that you should note.

1. Special Studies for Children

The term "Special Studies for Children" is a term chosen to designate certain new Covenant Life Curriculum resources for children developed for use on a variety of possible occasions outside the regular systematic study of the school.

These studies, which are based on the same Biblical and educational principles as the regular studies, are planned as a part of the total program of Christian education for children and are to be administered through the regular church school structure.

These courses, which are flexible in design, are suited for use in a variety of ways. They may be used in the schedule that has been familiar in the vacation church school, but their use is by no means limited to this kind of setting. Other possible occasions would be certain weekdays or Saturday mornings arranged over a period of time, one or two days a week during the summer, and church family nights when adults and youth are also engaged in study. Each church should build its own program to fit the needs of its own children, keeping in mind the resources available.

2. Youth in the Church

Your committee is responsible for oversight not only of the systematic study program for youth but also of the additional activities which the church provides for its young people. There is a new approach to youth work in the church with which your committee should be familiar.

In the Covenant Life Curriculum there is a strong emphasis on youth as responsible members of the church. The training of youth for responsible membership is an aim of the studies designed for them in the school of the church and also of special materials developed for use in preparing young people for communicant membership. It is to be hoped that young people will be given an opportunity to participate more fully with adults in the life and work of the church through serving with adults on committees and working with them in specific church enterprises.

There will be many occasions outside their regular classes for systematic study when youth will want to meet as a youth group to pursue special concerns and interests resulting from their study or from issues raised in daily life. Resources are being provided to meet such needs, and it is recommended that the youth structure in the school of the church serve as the organization through which additional activities for this age group will be planned.

The new approach to youth work provides an opportunity for young people and their leaders to work together with more understanding and effectiveness. The members of your committee will want to become familiar with this approach as it is reflected and described in the youth manual.[5]

3. Camps and Conferences

Camps and conferences provide an important element in the total program of Christian education, and it will be well for your committee to know what they provide for young people of different ages.

For seventh and eighth graders, camps of five to twelve days duration are planned as a part of the summertime outdoor Christian education program. These are usually presbytery-sponsored but may be planned by a church or a group of churches. The living situation, stripped of most of the commercialisms of the day and making the camper dependent on the group for much of the program, offers a unique opportunity for study and interpersonal relationships under mature Christian leadership. The elements of the world about the campers serve as a means for teaching man's relation to God, the Creator and Sustainer, and man's relationship to man.

---

5. Betsy Rice, *Youth in the Church* (Richmond: The CLC Press, 1963).

For ninth graders, the camping experience is combined with a more concentrated study of the theme, God's call to the individual for dedication in his life's work. The setting and group relationships are important as teaching media.

Camping for tenth, eleventh, and twelfth graders may continue on the presbytery campsite, with the campers being responsible for most of their meals as well as for developing their program of study and activities. This age group may come together at the site for two days of orientation and then go off on a trailer, canoe, back-packing, or bicycle camping trip in smaller groups.

The conference program is designed particularly for tenth through twelfth graders. Three Bible study courses will be provided, with suggestions to lead into a consideration of churchmanship and personal Christian growth. The youth booklets and other current materials may be used as supplements where a wider variety is desired.

Leadership Training

The general enlistment of leaders is the responsibility of the Committee on Commitment, but the responsibility for seeing that proper arrangements are made for training of leaders for various programs of the church, as well as for the school of the church, is yours. The manual, *The Development of Leaders for the School of the Church*,[6] as well as the Resource Guide on Strengthening the Church, will offer your committee valuable guidance.

1. Elders and Deacons

The Book of Church Order requires that a period of training be given for persons elected to the office of Ruling Elder and Deacon (§ 29-2). This should include courses in the system of doctrine, government, and discipline of our Church as well as the

---

6. Sara Little, *The Development of Leaders for the School of the Church* (Richmond: The CLC Press, 1965).

duties of the office to which each has been elected. Books you will want to use include *The Confession of Faith, The Book of Church Order,* and *The Work of the Church—Whose Responsibility?* along with *The Noble Task* (for Elders) and *Chosen to Serve* (for Deacons).

2. *Other Designated Leaders*

Your church will have a variety of leaders who will serve in visiting, teaching, administration, planning, and so on. It will be your responsibility to see that all of these leaders receive training. The task of leader education may be assigned to the particular organizations or groups to be served by the leaders, or the responsibility for training all leaders in the church may be given to the school of the church. If the latter alternative is chosen, an assistant superintendent may be named to direct an over-all plan of leader training. In any case, all leadership development should be co-ordinated under your committee into a single program. Helps for training leaders are available from the various Boards and Agencies of the Church and from the Presbyterian Book Stores.

Developing Responsible Churchmen

In strengthening the local church for its work, another important educational task of your committee is to help your congregation grow in its understanding of the Church. This will include such things as a study of the meaning of the sacraments, the congregational order of worship, learning about your hymnbook, studying the meaning of church architecture, and learning about Presbyterian government, which would include a study of the courts of the Church, congregational meetings, and the like. Consult the Resource Guide on Strengthening the Church which will be found in your annual *Presbyterian Plan Book* for ideas and suggestions for developing such an educational program.

Developing a Supportive Fellowship

Why would fellowship be included under this committee?

Because your job is to strengthen the church in its work through education. As we fellowship together we are learning. We are learning about the meaning of our common relationship to Christ within our particular fellowship, and we learn as we have fellowship with other Christians across congregational, denominational, and national lines.

1. Fellowship Within Your Own Congregation

Perhaps the fellowship within your own congregation would best be handled by the Committee on Service, which is responsible for congregational care. However, your committee can work with them in developing such things as neighborhood fellowships that engage in Bible study, service of some kind, or meetings for prayer and fellowship together. Other ideas you might use in co-operation with the Committee on Service include family recreation, recreation for special occasions (family night, picnics, parties, etc.), and planning events for special groups (such as the aged, persons who must work on Sunday, single adults, and so on).

2. Fellowship Within the Community

Fellowship among Christians of various denominations is possible through such organizations as United Church Women and the Council of Churches of your city. Encourage your people to participate. Such occasions as Reformation Sunday, World-Wide Communion Sunday, and the World Day of Prayer also may be a time of fellowship. Take advantage of these opportunities to get your people to participate in the wider Christian family of your community.

3. Fellowship Within the Courts of the Church

Additional opportunities for developing a broader fellowship are to be found within the presbytery, synod, and General Assembly. This happens by encouraging participation in the various camp, leadership, and training programs. Our faith becomes more meaningful to us as we meet and get to know others of like faith who share with us common hopes and dreams in our witness to Jesus Christ.

4. Other Opportunities

There are many other ways that your committee can develop to create a supportive fellowship. Encourage reading of the official publications of the courts of the Church as well as the independent papers and magazines that treat religious matters. Plan joint services with other groups, and encourage your people to be interested in the events of other denominations. Remember that our Church belongs to the National Council of Churches, the World Council of Churches, and the Presbyterian World Alliance. Help your people to become informed about these organizations and to have an interest and concern that is broader than their own congregation or denomination.

Other Duties

There will be many things that you will be called upon to do. You may be made responsible for such things as the church library or some special educational undertaking. Since "education" is a broad term, the major part of the work of the local church could conceivably be delegated to you. The important thing is to do the job well. Define your goals, establish your methods, select your leaders, delegate responsibility, and check on results. Yours is a difficult and demanding job.

A Concluding Statement

Perhaps more help is available for your committee than for any other. The offices of Christian Education of your presbytery and synod will help your committee in structuring its work and executing its plans. Do not hesitate to ask for help or to write for information, which is available for you in every area. You will discover that these various agencies are eager to assist you in any way.

This chapter has been limited, not because there is little to do but because there is so much that one chapter can hardly begin to reveal the opportunities for service. So much good material has been written that it would be useless to attempt to duplicate it here in abbreviated form. Perhaps this overview will give you a sufficiently broad perspective so that your committee can proceed intelligently. What can be done is unlimited. There is no lack of ideas, materials, and aids for your committee in almost any undertaking for Christian nurture and growth. The only limitation on the program of Strengthening the Church will be the willingness of your committee to plan, to study, and to work.

XII

THE NOBLE TASK

To be an Elder is no light responsibility. It will demand the best that you have to give. It will require of you time, faithfulness, application, and diligence. Yes, it will be work; but as someone has expressed it, God did not call us into His vineyard to eat grapes, but to hoe! Let us be workmen who need not be ashamed.

With a little better understanding of the scope of your duties, you have a starting point for the task that is yours. We have not begun to exhaust the possibilities open to you in the fulfilling of your responsibilities, but now you are on your own! It should be remembered that although there are many things you can do, you cannot do everything. It is far better to do a few things well than many things poorly. Survey the needs, consider the ways to meet those needs, and execute a well-planned, well-organized method of meeting each need. But remember—records, plans, ideas, organizations, are not an end in themselves. Your business is with persons and their spiritual welfare. If you are helping and serving people in meaningful areas of life in their spiritual pilgrimage, you are doing your job. If you are helping them in their relationship to Christ and His Church, if they are growing in favor with God and man, then all the work is worth while and the noble task is being done.

There is one final thing that should be said about the Session and its various committees. The Session is the policy-making body which directs future actions or activities. The committee is the executive body through which the work actually gets done. Thus, though we make all sorts of policies and rules and regulations, nothing will get done until it becomes a reality through the work of committees. Therefore, it is not enough that you be faithful and diligent in your attendance at meetings of the Session. You must be just as reliable in the executive functions of your committees.

Perhaps it would be well here at the last to say a word about your particular committee (whichever one it is) and the minister. He cannot possibly attend all of the committee meetings. Don't expect him to. Also, do not expect him to do your planning, to think up ideas for you and then to carry them out. Your job is to free him from the duties of *your* committee for the other duties that are especially *his*. Keep him informed of your activities, consult him for his advice and opinions, but require your committee to do its own work.

Remember, too, that not only must you plan *what* you want to do; but in order to make it a reality, you must also plan *how* it will be done and *who* will do it. So many committee meetings produce wonderful plans and ideas that die prematurely simply because the plans were not completed; the committee neglected to determine how and who.

Good things never just happen. This cannot be overemphasized; for it takes planning, organizing, and executing to have an adequate program in a local church. Therefore, every church should set aside some time during the fall of the year (perhaps in October) in which leaders within the church would sit down together to plan the program of the church for the coming year. Each year around the first of September there is available to you the *Presbyterian Plan Book,* to be secured from the Presbyterian Book Store near you. This book is prepared by the Program Committee of the General Council. It will be indispensable to you in planning your church program for the coming year. Using this book, the leaders of your church can plan for a more effective program and can give each part of the work of the church its proper emphasis. Make use of pre-planned calendars, such as those of the Women of the Church, Synod, and Presbytery. This will be one of the most rewarding things you can do in helping your church to co-ordinate its work and give each phase of its program an adequate emphasis. Also, it will enable you to co-ordinate your local church program with that of our denomination.

With the year's activities and plans laid out in advance, the Session can see that the plans are carried to completion. Your pre-planned calendar will serve as the basis for the monthly calendar to be mailed to your congregation. For example, by October of one year, plans should have been made for special services for Easter and Christmas of the next year. Things done at the last minute and without much planning are seldom successful. Let it not be so at your church!

For a book of this nature to be helpful, you will have to exercise discretion in what you use, wisdom in what you reject, and your imagination in what you add. It is our hope that having a grasp of the broad perspective of the task that belongs to the Session, you can go on from there.

The Presbyterian Church is a great Church. It is a great Church because her laymen have made it so. It is great because her form of government, ordained of God and set forth in Holy Scripture, provides a channel for its officers and people to work under the inspiration of the Holy Spirit. Our form of government does not burden us with a hierarchy but binds us to God. And within this great Church, we who are Elders have a high and holy task as we serve as undershepherds of the Master. Work, toil, labor—yes! But the goal for which we strive is worthy of the race. Indeed, "The saying is sure: If any one aspires to the office of bishop, he desires a noble task."

Appendix A

STANDARD OF PROCEDURE
THE SESSION

Subject to the provisions of the Book of Church Order, the Session of the First Presbyterian Church, 400 Main Street, Anywhere, U.S.A., shall organize itself and conduct its affairs according to the following Standard of Procedure.

I. OFFICERS

The officers of the Session shall be a Moderator, a Moderator Pro Tempore, and a Clerk.

II. DUTIES OF OFFICERS

A. THE MODERATOR

The Moderator shall convene and preside at all meetings of the Session; shall call meetings when he deems it necessary or when requested to do so under the conditions set forth in the Book of Church Order; shall, in conjunction with the permanent committee chairmen, name Session members to permanent (working) committees; shall report to the Session any problems, whether spiritual, administrative, or personal, which relate to the welfare of the church; and shall serve as advisory member of all committees of the Session, including temporary as well as permanent (working) and special Sessional committees.

B. THE CLERK

The Clerk shall keep minutes of all meetings and see to it that such minutes are approved and properly endorsed; shall make and keep records of all reports for Presbytery, Synod, and General Assembly; shall keep an up-to-date membership roll, including an accurate list of inactive members and non-communing members; shall take care of the necessary correspondence of the Session, including dismission of members; shall keep all records necessary, including committee reports; shall keep available at all meetings orders of procedure; shall notify all members of the Session of date, time, and place of meetings; shall remind and notify all committees, councils, persons, etc., of the actions taken by the Session pertaining to that group or person; shall keep an accurate and indexed reference of all motions and resolutions passed by the Session until such time as those motions or resolutions are no longer applicable; shall act as the Moderator's assistant at all meetings of the Session; shall issue baptismal and membership certificates to those who are baptized and/or received into the church; shall keep an accurate record of all baptisms, marriages, deaths, and other significant events.

C. THE MODERATOR PRO TEMPORE

The Moderator Pro Tempore shall act as Moderator during emergencies when the Moderator is absent or unable to act; shall act as Moderator when the church is without a pastor.

III. NOMINATIONS

At the October stated meeting of each year a nominating committee shall be elected by the Session, consisting of three Elders, one of whom shall be named chairman. At the November stated meeting of each year it shall be the duty of this committee to place in nomination names of Elders for Clerk, Moderator Pro Tempore, and chairmen for each permanent (working) committee and each special Sessional committee, having previously secured permission of such Elders. The minister shall serve as advisory member of the Nominating Committee.

IV. ELECTION OF OFFICERS
AND COMMITTEE CHAIRMEN

Officers and committee chairmen shall ordinarily be elected at the stated meeting in November of each year and shall assume office on the first of January of the following year. At the time of election the Nominating Committee shall report; and further nominations may be made from the floor. All terms of office coincide with the calendar year. No Elder shall ordinarily hold two elective offices. Elders-elect will be invited to attend the election and are eligible for appointment to office.

V. TERMS OF OFFICE

A. THE CLERK

The Clerk shall be elected for a term of one year. He shall not ordinarily succeed himself for more than three years.

B. THE MODERATOR PRO TEMPORE

The Moderator Pro Tempore shall be elected for a term of one year. He shall not ordinarily succeed himself for more than one year.

C. CHAIRMEN OF PERMANENT OR WORKING COMMITTEES

Chairmen of permanent (or working) committees shall be elected for a term of one year. Chairmen shall not ordinarily succeed themselves for more than three years.

D. CHAIRMEN OF TEMPORARY COMMITTEES

Chairmen of temporary committees shall be appointed or elected for the period necessary to fulfill their special responsibility, or for such time as the Session may designate.

E. CHAIRMEN OF SPECIAL SESSIONAL COMMITTEES

Chairmen of special Sessional committees shall be elected for a term of one year. Chairmen shall not ordinarily succeed themselves for more than three years.

VI. VACANCIES OR ABSENCES

When an elective office falls vacant, or when such officer is absent for an extended period, the Moderator shall have the authority to appoint persons temporarily to fill that office until an election can be held or until such time as the absent officer resumes his duties. In the case of a chairman of a committee, each committee shall have a vice-chairman who shall serve as chairman until the chairman returns or another chairman is elected by the Session.

VII. MEETINGS

The Session shall ordinarily meet on the third Monday of each month at 7:30 p.m. at the church unless, by majority vote at a regular stated meeting, the date, time, and place are changed. The Moderator may call special meetings at any time desired, provided sufficient notice of time and place is given, or when requested to do so under the provisions set forth in the Book of Church Order. No business which has not been clearly stated in the call shall ordinarily be considered at a special meeting. All meetings shall be opened and closed with prayer. Further, the Session shall have a joint meeting with the Board of Deacons at least twice a year, ordinarily in February and September, and at such times as the Session may consider advisable.

VIII. ATTENDANCE

Each member of the Session is morally bound to be present at all meetings unless providentially hindered. If a member of the Session is unable to be present at any meeting, he shall so notify the Clerk and present his excuse to the court through him.

IX. QUORUM

The quorum for all meetings of the Session shall consist of no fewer than eight members of the Session, except for the purpose of receiving members, in which case the quorum shall be the Moderator and two Elders. The quorum for a committee shall be one half the committee, provided that number be no less than two, one of whom must be either the chairman or vice-chairman.

X. COMMITTEES

A. PERMANENT OR WORKING COMMITTEES

The permanent or working committees of the Session shall be the following: Committee on Worship, Committee on Commitment, Committee on Witness, Committee on Service, and Committee on Strengthening the Church.

B. Temporary Committees

The Moderator may appoint, or the Session create, any necessary temporary committees to which may be assigned tasks not included in or related to the prescribed duties of permanent (working) committees or special Sessional committees. Temporary committees may be assigned duties falling under the responsibility of permanent (working) committees; but this may be done only upon recommendation of the permanent committee involved, unless the temporary committee is created by a three-fourths majority of the Session members present.

C. Special Sessional Committees

The special Sessional committees, created for duties to be performed by Session members only, shall include the following: Committee Relating to Work of Deacons; Committee Relating to Ordination and Installation of Church Officers; Committee Relating to Staff Members; Committee Relating to Other Church Courts; Committee Relating to Discipline.

XI. PERMANENT OR WORKING COMMITTEES

A. Committee on Worship

1. *Membership.* This committee shall have at least two Elders, who shall be chairman and vice-chairman. It shall have as advisory members a representative from the Ushering Committee of the Board of Deacons, the organist, the Director of Music, the Director of Christian Education, and the minister.

2. *Duties.* The Committee on Worship is responsible for the actual service of worship in all of its aspects. Its duties shall be to:

(1) Have charge of arrangements for Communion services, including serving shut-ins each quarter or at least annually on World-Wide Communion Sunday. This duty shall particularly include training of Elders for serving the sacrament.

(2) Have responsibility for co-ordinating the work of this committee with that of the organist, Director of Music, and any other personnel concerned with the music of the church.

(3) Hear a report monthly from the Director of Music and

work with him in securing new choir members, starting new choirs, etc., as the committee works with the Director of Music in creating a full musical program for the church.

(4) Co-operate with the Director of Music for all special musical programs.

(5) Deal with the worship of the church in terms of the order of worship, sanctuary appointments, aids to worship, special services, etc.

(6) Be responsible for supply pastors for special occasions and for times when the minister is absent.

(7) Recommend all policies concerning musical aspects of the church's program, including securing assistant or substitute musicians, in co-operation with the Director of Music.

(8) Recommend the policies to be followed in the use of buildings and musical instruments for weddings and other activities not in the stated program of the church.

(9) Initiate whatever means are necessary to develop a sense of reverence and worship among the congregation.

(10) Promote the program of music throughout the church.

(11) Be responsible for the development of the prayer life of the congregation, both collectively and individually.

(12) Be responsible for providing Elders with training toward supplying the pulpit. The names of those who are willing to serve in this way shall be made available to the Commission on the Minister and His Work of the Presbytery.

(13) Develop and maintain necessary rules and regulations to govern the conducting of funerals which shall serve as an aid to those who are bereaved.

(14) Develop and maintain necessary rules and regulations, along with other useful helps and aids, to be used in the conducting of weddings.

B. COMMITTEE ON COMMITMENT

1. *Membership.* This committee shall have at least two Elders, who shall be the chairman and vice-chairman. It shall have as ex officio members the chairman of the Budget Committee of the Board of Deacons and one other Deacon so appointed by the

Board, together with persons representing the other organizations of the church: men, women, youth, children, *et al.,* and members-at-large as needed and available. It shall have as advisory members the bookkeeper-treasurer and the minister.

2. *Duties.* Although the finances of the church are primarily the duty of the Board of Deacons, the Session's Committee on Commitment is responsible for the church's program of total commitment, of which finances are a part. Therefore, not only does the Committee on Commitment recommend to the Session *policies* concerning finances, it is also responsible for fitting the stewardship program of the Board into the over-all program of total commitment. Generally, the duties of this committee shall be to:

(1) Develop a program for deepening the commitment of time, abilities, and money of communing members.

(2) Develop a program of leading non-communing members to commitment to Jesus Christ through communicants' classes and other means.

(3) Develop a program of new member assimilation as well as a program to lead new members to a beginning commitment of time, abilities, and money. Such development may include a new members class and other suitable programs.

(4) Develop a method whereby the talents and abilities of the congregation may be discovered and used, as well as work with appropriate committees of the Session to train those who indicate a willingness to serve in particular areas.

(5) Challenge to full-time Christian service in church-related careers those who it feels are qualified and are being led by the Holy Spirit.

(6) Develop a program of study and training to help our members understand the meaning of Christian vocation and the call to church-related careers. Such program shall include the Vocational Guidance Program of our denomination for our youth.

(7) Work with the Board of Deacons to develop a year-round program of stewardship that will be an integral part of the committee's year-round program of total commitment.

(8) Relate to our congregation matters of interest and concern in other courts of the Church. This shall include the duty to recommend to the Session representatives to the meetings of Presbytery and Synod.

(9) Take the oversight of other organizations within the church such as the Women of the Church, Men of the Church, etc., and report to the Session the activities of these groups along with suggested policies and recommendations concerning them.

(10) Work with the Board of Deacons in terms of stewardship and commitment within the congregation, financial goals, and other special financial programs.

(11) Recommend to the Session policies relating to financial matters of the church, particularly in the field of benevolence stewardship.

(12) Promote continuous stewardship emphasis, in co-operation with the Board, as well as special seasons of stewardship.

(13) Have the responsibility for making a job analysis for each unordained staff member, in co-operation with the pastor and the Special Sessional Committee Relating to Staff Members.

(14) Make policy recommendations to the Session concerning activities where a fee is charged or which have the making of money as one object.

(15) Receive memorial and other gifts and see that these are properly acknowledged.

(16) Keep a memorial record book.

(17) Sponsor an annual memorial service in co-operation with the Committee on Worship.

(18) Make recommendations to the Session from time to time of suitable gifts to be purchased as memorials.

(19) Suitably inscribe memorial objects, designating donors or otherwise indicating the object as a memorial.

C. COMMITTEE ON WITNESS

1. *Membership.* This committee shall consist of at least two Elders, who shall be chairman and vice-chairman. It shall have persons representing the organizations of the church: Deacons, men, women, youth, children, *et al.,* together with members-at-

large as needed and available. It shall have as ex officio members the president and vice-president of any organizations which have evangelism as a primary objective. The minister shall be an advisory member.

2. *Duties.* The Committee on Witness is responsible for the outreach program of the church. This includes evangelism in the local church, the outreach through Church Extension in the homeland, as well as the witness for Christ in the entire world through World Missions. The duties of the committee shall be to:

(1) Be responsible for welcoming all visitors and guests to all services, working to create an atmosphere of friendliness and concern in the church members.

(2) Be responsible for devising ways and means of securing names of prospects through surveys, the "Ritual of Friendship," the church school, and other appropriate means, and for keeping an up-to-date prospect list.

(3) Be responsible for the visitation of the unchurched and unsaved with a view to leading them to Christ and to membership in the church.

(4) Sponsor and maintain a program of continuous visitation evangelism as well as sponsor special seasons of evangelism.

(5) Have the oversight of the work of any organizations whose primary objective is evangelism.

(6) Sponsor a continuous program of evangelism through the various organizations of the church, especially the church school, Men of the Church, and Women of the Church, using these organizations where possible as means of accomplishing the purpose of this committee.

(7) Co-operate with the Presbytery's Commission on the Minister and His Work in supplying destitute places with the regular ministry of the Word by providing the names of qualified Elders. In this connection, the committee shall work with the Committee on Worship in finding and developing such Ruling Elders.

(8) Recommend to the Session appropriate observance of the Church Extension and World Mission seasons in the church.

(9) Develop interest within the congregation in the extension program of our Presbytery, Synod, and General Assembly.

(10) Sponsor an annual School of Missions, keep the congregation informed on the activities of missionaries, and use any appropriate means to keep us aware of our missionary enterprise around the world, as well as to encourage and challenge those whom the committee feels are qualified to enter this service.

(11) Use any other ideas and programs that apparently would be useful to promote witnessing to our faith in Jesus Christ whether in our own church, our homeland, or around the world.

D. COMMITTEE ON SERVICE

1. *Membership.* This committee shall have at least two Elders, who shall be chairman and vice-chairman. It shall have persons representing the Women of the Church, the Men of the Church, and various other groups of the church: Deacons, youth, children, *et al.*, together with members-at-large as needed and available. It shall have as ex officio members the secretary of the church school and the president of any group which carries shepherding responsibilities for members of the congregation. It shall have as advisory members the Director of Christian Education and the minister.

2. *Duties.* This committee shall seek to interpret to the members of the congregation the meaning of Christian service and offer opportunity not only to serve others, but also to participate in Christian action against the evils of our society and the world. In addition, this committee shall seek to be the arm of pastoral care of the people for the Session. More specifically, such duties shall include the following:

(1) Have the responsibility for the attendance of the members at church functions, particularly attendance at services of divine worship. The committee shall use whatever means are deemed expedient in developing the habit of participation in services of worship and in the school of the church.

(2) Be responsible for the visitation of the sick, shut-ins, and bereaved.

(3) Have the general oversight of the congregation for its spiritual welfare, keeping careful watch that the flock entrusted to the care of the Session be not neglected.

(4) Be responsible for co-operating with the pastor to keep him informed of those who need his attention and to help him minister to their needs.

(5) Discover areas of need as well as groups or individuals that need the love and concern and help of our congregation, and lead our people in ministering to those needs in the name of Christ.

(6) Discover areas of evil that exist in our community and in the world, and lead our congregation in attacking these evils and removing the conditions that caused them.

(7) Work with any committee whenever called upon for publicity, information, and promotion.

(8) Be responsible for keeping a calendar of activities to inform the congregation regularly and systematically of the services and opportunities available to them within our church. This will include a monthly calendar of activities as well as the weekly announcement sheet, bulletin boards, etc.

(9) Keep the program of the church before the congregation by a monthly news sheet to interpret the program to the people.

(10) Be responsible for any special displays or equipment desired by any committee.

(11) Be responsible for an annual church planning conference for developing the program of the church for the following year. (This is the responsibility of the Committee on Planning and Research where such a committee exists.)

E. COMMITTEE ON STRENGTHENING THE CHURCH

1. *Membership.* This committee shall consist of at least two Elders, who shall be chairman and vice-chairman; the chairman of Home and Family Life; and representatives from the church at large, including youth. It shall have as advisory members the superintendent of the church school and such other persons as the committee may select to serve in an advisory capacity. The minister shall be an ex officio member. The Director of Chris-

tian Education shall serve as administrator of the committee.

2. *Duties.* This committee shall guide the church in its program to sustain and strengthen the members that they may effectively witness and serve. This shall include home and family nurture, systematic study, development of responsible churchmanship, training of effective leadership, and the development of a supportive fellowship. More specifically, it shall work to:

(1) Develop a program of home and family nurture for the members of the congregation which is appropriate for our church and which is recommended by our denomination through the Board of Christian Education.

(2) Develop a program of systematic study that best meets our needs and which shall include the following responsibilities:

(a) Determine the educational goals or objectives of the church school which serve as a basis upon which its program is projected.

(b) Nominate to the Session at its October stated meeting a superintendent and a secretary for the school of the church, to serve for the following year.

(c) Analyze and evaluate the program of the church school. Such study shall give a basis for building a program to strengthen and improve the present work in the light of the best educational goals, methods, and materials.

(d) Recommend the over-all policies of the church school in regard to activities of various groups, personnel, curriculum, housing, etc.

(e) Make plans for enlarging and increasing the effectiveness of the church school and provide ways of executing these plans.

(f) Select the curriculum materials for use in the church school.

(g) Survey continually the needs of the church school and plan for the necessary staff, working closely with the superintendent and the department heads. It shall maintain an up-to-date list of the staff of the church school who have been approved by the Session. All staff personnel shall be reviewed by the Session each year and approved for the following year. No person may be added to the approved list without the approval of the Session. Further, this committee shall work out long-range plans for meeting these needs, including plans for a program of training the staff.

(h) Work with the officers of the church and the church school to arrive at a suitable financial plan that will provide adequately for the systematic study program.

(i) Check housing and equipment and continually work toward providing better facilities for the school.

(j) Hear reports of the church school officers with regard to the condition of the school and convey these, together with a report of the committee's own actions and recommendations, to the Session.

(k) Maintain contact with the Board of Christian Education and other denominational agencies and seek to carry out their plans when possible.

(l) Encourage attendance at conferences, camps, meetings, training sessions, etc., and determine policies relating to attendance, finances, etc.

(m) Have the oversight of the Church School Council and its work.

(3) Provide leadership training courses when needed and as requested by other committees or groups.

(4) Provide an annual officer training course for Elders-elect and Deacons-elect.

(5) Be responsible for the oversight of any special educational undertakings of the church.

(6) Be responsible for the summer program of the church as it relates to the church school and the educational work.

(7) Have oversight of the church library.

(8) Undertake a program designed to develop responsible churchmen of our members through educational courses in the sacraments, worship, architecture, church government, and other significant areas.

(9) Be responsible for the general fellowship of the church in co-operation with the Board of Deacons.

(10) Develop a supportive fellowship within our own congregation through such means as Bible study groups, special interest groups, occupational groups, age groups, etc.

(11) Develop a broader supportive fellowship with Christians of other denominations in our own community through such organizations as are available and are approved by our Session.

(12) Develop a supportive fellowship that cuts across denominational, national, and community lines.

XII. COMMITTEE MEMBERSHIP AND OPERATION

A. Membership and Terms of Office

Every active Elder shall be appointed by the minister and the elected chairmen, with Sessional approval, to serve on a permanent (working) committee; and each committee, whether permanent (working) or temporary, shall have as its chairman and vice-chairman members of the Session. Each committee, with the consent of the Session, may appoint members from the congregation to serve on said committee, except in the case of special Sessional committees whose duties can be performed only by members of the Session. Members of the congregation appointed to a committee shall be so appointed for a term of one year or part thereof, term to expire with the calendar year. Ordinarily no person shall be asked to serve on a committee for more than three successive terms. The person so appointed shall be advised of the duties of the committee to which he is being appointed; and his name shall not be submitted for Sessional approval until he has consented to serve.

B. Meetings of Committees

Each committee shall ordinarily meet at least once monthly, at such time as called by the chairman or at the request of the Session. Ordinarily all committees of the Session shall meet together in January of each year for a general meeting for the purpose of training and orientation.

C. Reports

Each committee shall ordinarily make a monthly report to the Session at the regular stated meeting or when required to report by the Session. All committee recommendations and policies must be approved by the Session, which alone is responsible for the total program of the church.

D. Records

Each committee shall ordinarily keep an accurate record of its reports, minutes, and activities. These records are to be available to the Session upon request.

XIII. QUESTIONS OF PROCEDURE

All questions of procedure not covered herein or by the Book of Church Order shall be governed by *Robert's Rules of Order Revised*.

XIV. AMENDMENTS

This Standard of Procedure may be amended by a majority vote of those present at a regular stated meeting, provided the proposed amendment was presented in writing and approved by a majority vote at a previous stated meeting. Any part of this Standard of Procedure may be set aside by a three-fourths vote of those present at a stated meeting, providing the number constituting three-fourths of those present is not less than one half of the membership of the Session.

Appendix B

JOB ANALYSIS
DIRECTOR OF CHRISTIAN EDUCATION

LINES OF AUTHORITY

The Director of Christian Education shall be directly responsible to the Session of the church for program responsibilities, and as a member of the church staff he shall be responsible to the minister.

REPORTS

The DCE shall report periodically to the Session on the entire area under his responsibility.

AREAS OF RESPONSIBILITY

To the Minister

The DCE shall work closely with the minister in the planning and evaluation of the program of Christian Education.

To the Committee on Strengthening the Church

The DCE shall work with the chairman and other members of the Committee on Strengthening the Church in the execution of the committee's responsibilities as set forth in the Standard of Procedure of the Session.

To the Church School Superintendent

The DCE shall consult with the superintendent (or superintendents) about the program, policies, and personnel of the church school. He shall advise and support the superintendent in his duties as administrator and in his work with the Church School Council.

To Other Organizations

Women of the Church. He shall assist the Women of the

Church in such areas as they may desire, especially in areas that relate to the educational aspects of their work.

Men of the Church. He shall serve as adviser in areas relating to the educational aspects of the program as the men may request.

Youth Groups. He shall serve as resource person and adviser to adult leaders of youth groups and to youth officers.

Other Groups. He shall co-operate with other church organizations in the educational aspects of their work.

To Church School Workers

He shall act as supervisor, consultant, and "teacher of teachers" in both pre-service and in-service leader development. He shall consult with teachers on special problems and shall work with leading teachers in planning and conducting departmental meetings.

GENERAL RESPONSIBILITIES

1. The Director of Christian Education shall be responsible for the supervision of the church library and shall recommend to the Committee on Strengthening the Church policies for the library's operation, including the system of selecting and purchasing new books.

2. He shall work with and assist the Committee on Service, especially in the area of public relations.

3. He shall serve as adviser on committees of the Session if requested to do so.

4. He shall visit persons within the church school as this relates to his responsibilities—that is, new church school members, sick children, teachers, new families, as well as members of the church school.

GENERAL POLICIES

1. The Director of Christian Education preferably shall not teach regularly in the church school except in special cases, as in a leadership class or an occasional elective course taught for one quarter.

2. He shall not be expected to contact personally any persons for teaching jobs or related activities.

3. He shall not be a member of any church school class or other special group within the church, except with the advice and consent of the minister.

4. He shall observe reasonable office and other working hours as set by the minister and/or the Session.

5. He shall have at least one full day a week free from his responsibilities.

6. He shall have not less than two full weeks of vacation each year.

7. He may work in one Presbytery camp each summer.

8. He may attend one conference, seminar, or institute for his own enrichment each year.

9. He may serve in special training conferences, schools, etc., with the approval of the Session.

Appendix C

JOB ANALYSIS
CHURCH SCHOOL SUPERINTENDENT

ELECTION AND TERM OF OFFICE

The superintendent of the church school shall be elected by
the Session at an October meeting, on the recommendation of
the Committee on Strengthening the Church, for a term of one
year. The term shall be effective January 1, and the superintendent shall be eligible for re-election for a second term. There
shall always be an assistant or associate serving with him as a
potential successor.

RESPONSIBILITIES

The responsibilities of the superintendent shall be:

1. As an ex officio member of the Committee on Strengthening the Church.

2. As the administrator of the school of the church.

3. As the chairman of the Church School Council.

The work of the superintendent is usually thought of as being
administrative.

He is responsible for seeing that the Church School Council,
under the guidance of the Committee on Strengthening the
Church, carries out its duties regarding personnel, space, equipment, and supply needs of the church school.

His office is concerned with:

1. Getting the program organized and in operation.

2. Seeing that personnel are provided and are properly
trained. He should nominate to the Session, through its Committee on Strengthening the Church, all associate and assistant
superintendents and division chairmen, and upon their recommendation all other personnel of the school for the Session's
election.

3. Seeing that properly selected and approved curriculum materials and supplies are used.

4. Making sure that groups are properly placed and that adequate equipment is provided.

5. Planning and calling meetings of the Council.

6. Planning for the keeping of accurate and full records.

7. Interpreting the program to the Session of the church and securing moral and financial support for the school program.

8. Seeing that other requirements for educational work of the church school are met.

A fuller discussion of the responsibilities of the superintendent is developed as we consider his several relationships to the church staff and personnel. (See also the manual *The School of the Church,* chapter 6, for further analysis of the responsibilities of the superintendent and of those who work with him.)

RELATIONSHIPS

To the Committee on Strengthening the Church

The superintendent is an advisory member of the Committee on Strengthening the Church. He will report, either personally or in writing, to that committee at each of its stated meetings. This shall include such matters as enrollment, attendance, and finances. Even more important, his report shall concern the quality of the educational program, including such matters as teachers, teaching methods, curriculum, and equipment. Such matters shall be discussed, recommendations adopted, and the whole passed on to the Session.

Through the Church School Council he shall administer and supervise the entire program of the church school, under the direction of the Session and its Committee on Strengthening the Church.

To the Church School Council

The superintendent is the chairman of the Church School Council. The Council is essential to every church school, regardless of size, and should include the following:

The school superintendent, as chairman; the associate superintendent; the assistant superintendents, if the school is large enough to need one or more of these; the four division chairmen (of the Preschool, Elementary, Youth, and Adult Divisions); and the pastor. The Minister of Education, or Director of Christian Education, should also be a member. When not more than ten or twelve persons are on the school staff, including officers and teachers, all of these should be on the Council.

The Church School Council should meet regularly—preferably each month—and all persons who are included in its membership should be aware of their responsibilities and have a clear understanding of the function and scope of the work of the Council. The duties of the Council include the following:

1. To co-ordinate the four divisions and their work.

2. To be responsible for personnel, space, equipment, and supply needs of the divisions.

3. To report regularly to the Session, through the superintendent and the Committee on Strengthening the Church, concerning the church school and its program.

4. To interpret and carry out plans of the Session conveyed through the superintendent.

5. To establish, in accord with the Session, policies for the qualifications and preparation of leaders; for the purchase and distribution of curriculum materials; and for the selection of curriculum material when alternative programs of study are offered.

6. To be responsible for educational and inspirational meetings of the entire school staff, as needed.

7. To see that its policies are interpreted to the division councils and are carried out satisfactorily. The division councils should be required to report regularly.

8. To approve, and recommend to the Committee on Strengthening the Church, the spending budget of the church school.

To the Pastor

In the Presbyterian Church, the pastor has as one of his primary duties to oversee the educational program of the church

(§ 10-4). The pastor as the Teaching Elder is the overseer of the total educational program of the church. He may delegate specific phases of this responsibility to a Director of Christian Education. For this reason, the superintendent will naturally look to the pastor for advice and counseling. This working relationship is essential to the life and effective administration of the church school. He will keep the pastor informed of the progress and needs of the school. The pastor can be of valuable help in the area of filling vacancies and advising on major changes in the program.

To the Director of Christian Education

Only about 10 percent of our churches have directors. This worker is an employed member of the church staff and has a responsibility for the entire educational program of the church.

The superintendent and Director of Christian Education are co-workers; neither has authority over the other, and both are responsible for making the school as fruitful as possible. The director should plan with the superintendent for meetings of the Church School Council.

The Director of Christian Education should be able to supply the superintendent with many helpful materials and suggestions for his program.

(Note: It is suggested that the superintendent study the job analysis of the director, so that he may know the specific responsibilities which the Session has given to this person.)

To Other Associates

The number of additional associates with whom the superintendent will work depends upon the scope of the work of the church school, and upon the policy set up by the Committee on Strengthening the Church in an effort to provide an adequate organization for the church school. There may be one or more associate superintendents if the school is large. All schools will need assistant superintendents and division chairmen. (An analysis of the responsibilities of these officers is given in *The School of the Church*.)

At all times at least one assistant or associate superintendent shall be in training to succeed the superintendent when the time comes. This person should be nominated to the Session by the Committee on Strengthening the Church, for election at least one full year before the expiration of the superintendent's final term. Election by the Session shall take place at an October meeting.

In emergencies, an associate shall be nominated by the Committee on Strengthening the Church and elected by the Session as quickly as possible, to fill an unexpired term of the superintendent.

The Church School Secretary shall be elected annually by the Committee on Strengthening the Church, to serve for one year. The term shall be effective January 1, and the secretary shall be eligible for a second term.

The secretary's duties shall be as follows:

1. To compile the school records and make them available to members of the staff who can profit by their use.

2. To prepare the record of attendance and offerings each Sunday morning, posting totals on the register. The offerings shall be given to the church treasurer each week, with statement indicating date and amount of church school offering.

3. To serve as recording secretary of the Church School Council and to keep permanent minutes of each meeting. She shall give the superintendent reminders and memorandums of items on which he will need to follow through. She shall keep a record of committee appointments and shall notify persons of their appointment when the superintendent asks her to do so.

4. She shall contact members of the Church School Council prior to meetings, informing them of date, time, and place of meeting.

Appendix D

JOB ANALYSIS
DIRECTOR OF MUSIC AND ORGANIST

LINES OF AUTHORITY

The Director of Music

The Director of Music shall be directly responsible to the Session of the church, and as a member of the church staff he shall be responsible to the minister. His work shall be carried on in co-operation with the Committee on Worship.

The Organist

The organist shall be directly responsible to the Session; immediately responsible to the Director of Music as his work relates to the choir; and immediately responsible to the minister in relation to the other parts of the service of worship and as a staff member.

GENERAL DUTIES

The Director of Music

1. Shall train and maintain an adult choir to be known as the Chancel Choir. Through this choir he shall carry on the ministry of choral music at services of worship.

2. Shall initiate and train other choirs as need or opportunity arises, giving special emphasis to youth and junior choirs.

3. Shall co-operate with other church groups in providing a ministry of music.

4. Shall co-operate with the superintendent of the church school in providing piano players for various classes, upon request.

5. Shall co-operate with the superintendent of the church school in working with the program of music in the church school, upon request.

6. Shall co-operate with the minister in making the program of choral music an integral part of the services of worship.

7. Shall make an effort to provide vocal music for special programs and services of worship, upon request.

8. Shall, for special occasions, provide a choral program in co-operation with the Committee on Worship. Ordinarily such occasions will be special services of music for Easter and Christmas, and others as requested by the committee.

9. Shall co-operate with the Committee on Worship in the continuous program of enlistment of singers and other musicians.

10. Shall offer to Chancel Choir members the opportunity for voice improvement and help in learning to read music.

11. Shall, with the consent and co-operation of the Committee on Worship and the minister, initiate whatever means are necessary to improve the quality of music in the life of the congregation and in the service of worship.

12. Shall be responsible for the proper care of choir robes, stoles, and other such equipment, as well as the proper care of the church library of choral music.

The Organist

1. Shall play for all regular services of worship.

2. Shall play for all regular rehearsals of the Chancel Choir.

3. Shall, from time to time and upon request of the Committee on Worship, present special services of organ music.

4. Shall co-operate with the minister and the Director of Music in making music an integral part of the services of worship.

5. Shall be responsible for the proper care of the church library of organ music.

GENERAL POLICIES

Weddings. Since only the organist is authorized to play the organ, he shall play for all weddings unless some acceptable organist is granted permission by the Session upon recommendation of the organist. A minimum fee should be established, to be paid directly to the organist by the wedding party.

Extra Services. In providing extra services of organ or choral music, both the organist and Director of Music shall be paid for such additional time. It shall be the duty of the Session to make such requests; and they shall also be responsible for determining the amount of additional remuneration by agreement of all parties concerned.

Vacation. Both the organist and the Director of Music shall have a two weeks' vacation for each year and shall be paid for such vacation. It shall be the duty of the Director of Music, in co-operation with the Session, to provide supply personnel for such absences. Further, the Session shall be responsible for determining the dates of vacations, fitting them into the program of the church.

Musical Supplies. The Committee on Worship shall provide a part of its budget for music supplies for both the organist and the Director of Music. Such music shall become a part of the music library of the church. Both the organist and the Director of Music shall have discretionary powers in the expenditure of that part of the budget designated for them; but the report of such expenditures shall be made to the Committee on Worship. Further, such request for funds for music shall be made through the proper channels established by the Board of Deacons.

Conferences and Training Schools. The Committee on Worship shall attempt to make available to the organist and Director of Music necessary fees for attending special music conferences and training schools. Both the organist and Director of Music shall make a special effort to attend one such school each year, such time not to be charged against their vacation time.

Appendix E

NEW MEMBER ASSIMILATION SHEET

FIRST SIX MONTHS

_____19____

MONTH:					
RATING:					

Record of Progress

G - good   P - poor   F - fair

1. Name _____

2. Address _____ Zip Code_____ Phone_____

3. Family Composition

	NAME	DATE OF BIRTH	DATE JOINED	HOW JOINED
Husband	_____	_____	_____	_____
Wife	_____	_____	_____	_____
Children	_____	_____	_____	_____
	_____	_____	_____	_____
	_____	_____	_____	_____

4. Job Information

	OCCUPATION	EMPLOYER
Husband	_____	_____
Wife	_____	_____

5. Family History Information _____

_____

_____

6. General Check List

_____New Member Packet
_____"Near Family" assigned. Name _____
_____Visit by pastor
_____Visit by DCE
_____Orientation session
_____Information Forms completed
_____Visit by Session
_____Entered on Permanent Roll
_____Letter from pastor sent

7. Organization Activation: Record of Notification

NAME	DATE SENT	DATE RETURNED	ATTENDING
Preschool Division			
Elementary Division			
Youth Division			
Westminster Fellowship			
Adult Class 1			
Adult Class 2			
Adult Class 3			
Adult Class 4			
Women of the Church			
Men of the Church			
Scouts			
Choir			

8. Final Check:

_____Has new member pledged?
_____Attending church regularly?
_____Attending the school of the church?
_____Attending other organizations?
_____Active in any phase of the church's work?
_____Need special attention? (If so, in what way?)_____
_____Should be referred to Session?

Appendix F

MONTHLY CALENDAR OF ACTIVITIES

722 Main Street

FIRST PRESBYTERIAN CHURCH
Anywhere, U.S.A.

John Smith, Minister

NOVEMBER—STEWARDSHIP AND EVERY MEMBER CANVASS

SUNDAY	MONDAY	TUESDAY	WEDNESDAY	THURSDAY	FRIDAY	SATURDAY
1962						1962
REGULAR SUNDAY SCHEDULE 8:45 a.m. Family Worship 9:30 a.m. Church School 11:00 a.m. Worship Service 5:00 p.m. Youth Recreation 6:00 p.m. Youth Supper, Program 7:30 p.m. Worship Service	REGULAR MONDAY SCHEDULE	REGULAR TUESDAY SCHEDULE	REGULAR WEDNESDAY SCHEDULE 7:00 a.m. Morning Prayers and Breakfast 6:30 p.m. Andrew and Good Shepherd Clubs 7:30 p.m. Chancel Choir	**1**	**2** WORLD COMMUNITY DAY	**3**
4	**5**	**6** 10:00 a.m.— WOC Exec. Board & Bible Study 7:30 p.m.— Boy Scouts	**7**	**8**	**9**	**10**
11 DEDICATION (EMC) DAY	**12** 7:30 p.m.— Deacons' Stated Meeting	**13** 10:30 a.m.— WOC Circles 6:30 p.m.— WOC Circles 7:30 p.m.— Boy Scouts	**14**	**15**	**16** 7:30 p.m.— Berean Class Meeting	**17**
			EVERY MEMBER CANVASS COMPLETION WEEK—November 11-18			
18 HOMES SUNDAY	**19** 7:30 p.m.— Session's Stated Meeting	**20** 11:00 a.m.— WOC General Program & Lunch 7:30 p.m.— Boy Scouts	**21**	**22** THANKSGIVING	**23** 7:00 p.m.— Women's Bible Class Meeting	**24**
				WORLD-WIDE BIBLE READING SEASON November 22—December 25		
25 EVANGELISM SUNDAY	**26**	**27** 7:00 p.m.— Men's Meeting 7:30 p.m.— Boy Scouts	**28**	**29**	**30**	

Appendix G

CHART A-1

POSSIBLE ORGANIZATION OF A SESSION

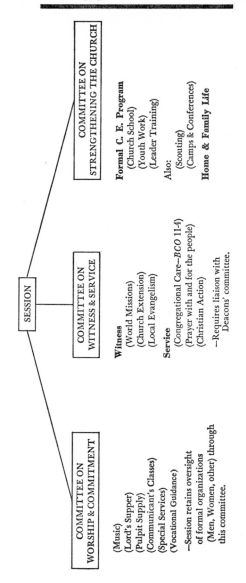

SESSION

COMMITTEE ON WORSHIP & COMMITMENT

(Music)
(Lord's Supper)
(Pulpit Supply)
(Communicant's Classes)
(Special Services)
(Vocational Guidance)

—Session retains oversight of formal organizations (Men, Women, other) through this committee.

COMMITTEE ON WITNESS & SERVICE

Witness
(World Missions)
(Church Extension)
(Local Evangelism)

Service
(Congregational Care—*BCO* 11-4)
(Prayer with and for the people)
(Christian Action)

—Requires liaison with Deacons' committee.

COMMITTEE ON STRENGTHENING THE CHURCH

Formal C. E. Program
(Church School)
(Youth Work)
(Leader Training)

Also:
(Scouting)
(Camps & Conferences)

Home & Family Life

NOTE A—Items **in bold type** on charts possibly require separate or subcommittees.

NOTE B—In the nominating, training, examining, ordaining and installing of Church Officers the Session's responsibility is determined by the *Book of Church Order*.

CHART A-2

POSSIBLE ORGANIZATION OF A SESSION

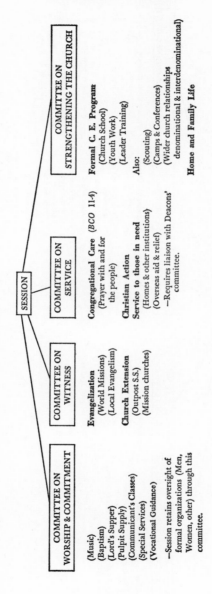

SESSION

COMMITTEE ON WORSHIP & COMMITMENT

(Music)
(Baptism)
(Lord's Supper)
(Pulpit Supply)
(Communicant's Classes)
(Special Services)
(Vocational Guidance)

—Session retains oversight of formal organizations (Men, Women, other) through this committee.

COMMITTEE ON WITNESS

Evangelization
(World Missions)
(Local Evangelism)

Church Extension
(Outpost S.S.)
(Mission churches)

COMMITTEE ON SERVICE

Congregational Care *(BCO* 11-4)
(Prayer with and for the people)

Christian Action
Service to those in need
(Homes & other institutions)
(Overseas aid & relief)
—Requires liaison with Deacons' committee.

COMMITTEE ON STRENGTHENING THE CHURCH

Formal C. E. Program
(Church School)
(Youth Work)
(Leader Training)

Also:
(Scouting)
(Camps & Conferences)
(Wider church relationships denominational & interdenominational)

Home and Family Life

NOTE A—Items **in bold type** on charts possibly require separate or subcommittees.

NOTE B—In the nominating, training, examining, ordaining and installing of Church Officers the Session's responsibility is determined by the *Book of Church Order.*

CHART A-3

POSSIBLE ORGANIZATION OF A SESSION

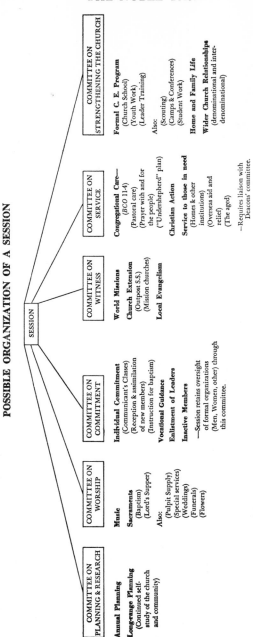

SESSION

COMMITTEE ON PLANNING & RESEARCH

Annual Planning

Long-range Planning
(*Continued self-study of the church and community*)

COMMITTEE ON WORSHIP

Music

Sacraments
(Baptism)
(Lord's Supper)

Also:
(Pulpit Supply)
(Special services)
(Weddings)
(Funerals)
(Flowers)

COMMITTEE ON COMMITMENT

Individual Commitment
(Communicant's Classes)
(Reception & assimilation of new members)
(Instruction for baptism)

Vocational Guidance

Enlistment of Leaders

Inactive Members

—Session retains oversight of formal organizations (Men, Women, other) through this committee.

COMMITTEE ON WITNESS

World Missions

Church Extension
(Outpost S.S.)
(Mission churches)

Local Evangelism

COMMITTEE ON SERVICE

Congregational Care—
(*BCO* 11-4)
(Pastoral care)
(Prayer with and for the people)
("Undershepherd" plan)

Christian Action

Service to those in need
(Homes & other institutions)
(Overseas aid and relief)
(The aged)

—Requires liaison with Deacons' committee.

COMMITTEE ON STRENGTHENING THE CHURCH

Formal C. E. Program
(Church School)
(Youth Work)
(Leader Training)

Also:
(Scouting)
(Camps & Conferences)
(Student Work)

Home and Family Life

Wider Church Relationships
(denominational and inter-denominational)

NOTE A—Items **in bold type** on charts possibly require separate or subcommittees.

NOTE B—In the nominating, training, examining, ordaining and installing of Church Officers the Session's responsibility is determined by the *Book of Church Order.*